C000178711

To dear Samara,

To remind you of me
and our many Christmases
together. Thank you for
being such a wonderful
sister.

With all my love,

Elanor
xxx

The A to Z
of Christmas

The A to Z of Christmas

Arnold Kellett

All rights reserved. No part of this publication may be reproduced, stored in a retrieval system, or transmitted, in any form or by any means, electronic, mechanical, photocopying or otherwise, without the prior permission of the publisher, Inspire.

Copyright © Arnold Kellett
Illustrations by Gordon Monaghan

British Library Cataloguing in Publication data
A catalogue record for this book is available
from the British Library

ISBN 1-85852-318-4
ISBN 978-1-85852-317-7

First published 2006 by Inspire
4 John Wesley Road
Werrington
Peterborough PE4 6ZP

Printed and bound in Great Britain by Stanley L Hunt (Printers) Ltd, Rushden, Northants.

Acknowledgements

In order to feel I have had the right atmosphere, all the research and writing for this book has been done during the Christmas period, that is, during Advent and the Twelve Days of Christmas. Not in one particular year, of course, but over forty years or so, as I have added bit by bit to my knowledge of this, the greatest religiously-inspired social phenomenon the world has ever seen.

So it follows that I am grateful to the many people who have contributed to my experience of the festive season. First, my parents, who all those years ago introduced my little brother and me to the wonders of Christmas. Can anything equal the thrill of waking up in the dark hours of Christmas morning to feel that magic burden on the bed? In later teenage years there were the Methodist friends with whom I went round our village carol singing from midnight on Christmas Eve, including Pat, the girl I married.

On rare occasions our carol singing was in the incomparable setting of a white Christmas, with everything transfigured by an immaculate blanket of sparkling snow. But Christmas transcends all weather conditions and the hottest tropical climate...

After army service including two Christmases in the Far East – and a Christmas dinner on the turbulent Bay of Biscay, on my way home – I eventually settled down to family life, sharing with Pat the joy of Christmas with our four children... all those nerve-racking visits from Santa Claus, when they were allowed, at some unearthly hour, to open their presents, but only when they heard my father give the signal by striking up with 'Christians, awake!' on the piano.

In later years, although the splendid meals and treats have continued as before, what matters most is that we are able to enjoy Christmas vicariously through our fifteen grandchildren.

So to all our family and friends who have helped to make our Christmas I dedicate this book, and hope it might help others experience, as I do, a delight undiminished by the passing years.

Special thanks are due, not only to Pat for her unfailing support, but to one of our graduate grandchildren, Molly, a young Christmas enthusiast, who has carefully checked both typescript and proofs.

Copyright Acknowledgements

Inspire gratefully acknowledges the use of copyright items. Every effort has been made to trace copyright owners, but where we have been unsuccessful, we would welcome information which would enable us to make appropriate acknowledgement in any reprint.

Plate 1: © The National Gallery, London. Used by permission.
Plate 2: © 2006 The Provost and Scholars of King's College, Cambridge. Used by permission.
Plate 4: Top © Arnold Kellett, Bottom © Norma Lackenby
Plate 5: © Arnold Kellett
Plate 6: © Arnold Kellett
Plate 7: Charles Wesley image courtesy of the Methodist Studies Unit, Oxford Brookes University
Plate 8: © PA/EMPICS. Used by permission.
Plate 11: © Royal Mail Group plc. Used by permission. All rights reserved.
Plate 12: © Arnold Kellett
Plate 14: © LiquidLibrary
Plate 15: Image provided Courtesy of Anand Kapoor at Image Foundry Studios www.imagefoundry.co.uk and Caroline Wilkinson Manchester University. Image Copyright © Image Foundry Studios'
Plate 16 © 2001 He Qi.

A Taste of Christmas Trifle

Before you start browsing through the following A to Z items, or look up some topic that particularly interests you, here, by way of introduction, is my 'Christmas Trifle'.

The idea is simply to set out the context into which all these various items fit, and at the same time help you to appreciate the evolution of Christmas from its primitive beginnings into this astonishing amalgam of religion, history, folklore, tradition, gastronomy, charity, social convention, commercial exploitation, and so much else.

It goes without saying that Christmas is not one thing, but many. Not simply a celebration of the birth of Christ, but a vast, international bean-feast of increasing complexity and magnitude, now so big that it is almost unmanageable, the supreme, compulsory festival which forces itself upon us year after year, dominating the lives of countless millions – and not just for the two or three days when Christmas is officially held, but for a build-up of weeks, and even many months.

My 'Christian Trifle' is the visual aid I always use to illustrate talks and lectures on the origin and development of Christmas. Its purpose is to show the various layers of which Christmas is composed, starting at the bottom with the oldest. Picture a glass bowl through the sides of which you can see the different layers of the trifle as they are added. This is how we can think of Christmas.

1. The Prehistoric Layer

Dark, spongy cake will do for this, sprinkled with spirits, perhaps, to suggest a mysterious, ancient flavour. This layer takes us back into the remotest past. It answers the question: Why do we celebrate the birth of Jesus in the depth of winter, when there is no hint in the Gospels that he was born at this time?

To understand why this part of the year was so important to our earliest ancestors – certainly those living in the northern hemisphere – we need to remember how filled with dread these days must have been. In modern times we are so cushioned from the harsh reality of winter by our comfortable homes, electric light, central heating, a secure food supply and so on, that it is difficult for us to comprehend the terror which must have seized the minds of primitive peoples as the year drew to its close. We call it the winter solstice, and explain it in terms of the rotation of the earth and its revolution round the sun. All *they* knew was that the days were getting shorter and shorter, the nights longer and colder. Each day the sun was lower in the sky, apparently growing weaker and weaker, and it really must have seemed that the sun itself was dying.

1

So in prehistoric times they devised various ceremonies intended to revive the dying sun, held around the time of the solstice, the 21 or 22 December. Because their ceremonies apparently worked – for soon the sun was seen to start climbing higher and higher in the sky, recovering its strength – they were repeated year after year at the same time.

These prehistoric rituals involved sacrifice, possibly even human sacrifice, and especially fire, making them festivals of light. A link with these ancient days can be seen in such winter solstice festivals as the Burning of the Clavie, various customs involving fires and flames, even the old game of snapdragon and the blazing brandy on the Christmas pudding. Psychologically at least, the Prehistoric Layer is still with us in the feeling that Christmas, at its absolute minimum, is a way of brightening up the gloomiest part of winter.

2. The Pagan Layer
Once we enter recorded history we find evidence of this winter solstice ceremonial still being performed, only now as part of the more formal religion of civilized nations. It was at the time of the solstice that the priests of the Celtic peoples, the Druids, cut the sacred mistletoe. The continuation of the fire symbolism is seen in the festival of Yule, observed both by the Anglo-Saxons and the Scandinavians, with the burning of the yule-log, kindled by a remnant of the log from the previous year, to ensure the continuity of life.

Most important of all was the Roman festival of Saturnalia, a lively midwinter carnival of evergreen decorations, exchanged presents, eating, drinking and making merry; and the celebration of the Unconquered Sun on the 25 December. So many features of Roman revelry, including this particular day, were eventually taken over by Christians, so that this is still one of the most strongly-flavoured layers in our Christmas Trifle.

3. The Christian Layer
While the pagan Romans were feasting and drinking in honour of their many gods and goddesses, there existed on the eastern fringe of their empire the nation of Israel, utterly opposed to polytheism and idolatry. Their prophets, such as Isaiah, had looked forward to the time when the Almighty would reveal himself by sending the Anointed One – in Hebrew *Messiah*, in Greek *Christos*. Christians believe that this prophecy was fulfilled when Jesus was born in Bethlehem, as described in the Gospel accounts of Luke and Matthew, with an interpretation of the significance of the birth in the Gospel of John.

How, then, did a monotheistic religion, with the lofty theology of Jesus as the Christ, the Son of God and Saviour of the world, come to be mixed up with a Roman polytheistic festival? Suggested explanations are given in the entry 'Christmas', but, whatever the reason, by the middle of the fourth century, in the western Church, the 25 December was being observed as the Feast of the Nativity, Christmas Day.

4. The Medieval Layer

This was a period, especially in the early years, when there was a consolidation of the pagan festive customs that had been retained but given a new Christian symbolism. There was the use of holly, for example, and even mistletoe, though unlike holly, you will find little mention of this in early carols and records, because of its especially strong pagan associations. The Church now found it necessary, amidst all the feasting and merrymaking, the tournaments and entertainments, to draw attention to the essential reason for Christmas, which is why St Francis, in the thirteenth century, encouraged the setting up of nativity scenes and the singing of carols. In England, as the medieval period merged into that of the Tudors, the richness and variety of food and drink was increasingly important at Christmas, at least for the wealthy.

5. The Puritan Layer

This layer of our trifle, paradoxically, will have to be something non-edible: a network of barbed wire, perhaps. It represents the fact that the Puritans under Oliver Cromwell, reacting to the excessive self-indulgence of earlier times, went so far as to outlaw the celebration of Christmas. Like the Jehovah's Witnesses of today, they argued that there is no mention of the festival in the Bible, and stridently dismissed it as a Catholic and 'Popish' invention. Fortunately, the Puritan Parliament's grim-faced abolition of Christmas lasted only until the Restoration of Charles II in 1660, both in Britain and in the American colonies.

6. The Victorian Layer

This is undoubtedly the thickest and richest of all the layers in the Christmas Trifle, marking an outstanding contribution both to the content and style of Christmas as we know it today. Although, following the Restoration, Christmas was celebrated once more, during the course of the eighteenth century it tended to be fairly low-key, with the emphasis on church services. In the nineteenth century, however, starting with the accounts by the American, Washington Irving, of his visits to England, followed by the popular writings of Charles Dickens, and the personal example of Prince Albert and Queen Victoria, there was a conscious attempt to revive the celebration of Christmas, not just in church and chapel, but in festive, convivial gatherings of family and friends. Within a few years, during the 1840s, the Victorians saw the widespread introduction of Christmas trees, Christmas cards, Christmas crackers, new and newly translated Christmas carols and, from America, the children's own gift-bringer, Santa Claus.

Though there was still a scandalous contrast between the life of the rich and the poor, the Victorians saw Christmas as a time for generous giving to those in need and, in spite of their strait-laced image, it must be conceded that they provided us with some of the most colourful and imaginative ingredients of our modern festival.

7. The Commercial Layer

This final layer, the one representing modern additions, is neither the thickest, nor the richest. It could consist, as is usual in trifles, of a topping of real cream or, if you have the cynicism of a neo-Puritan, a layer of frothy, tasteless cream substitute.

The commercialization of Christmas is not new, and could be seen at least in early Victorian times. If society is busy sending cards, exchanging presents and preparing to feast, then shopkeepers and merchants are bound to profit. But what is special about the last century or so is that mass production, sophisticated marketing and aggressive advertising, especially on television, have allowed Christmas to be commercially exploited on an unprecedented and phenomenal scale, so that is now the world's essential perennial money-spinner. For many consumers it has become little more than the annual festival of self-indulgence, a reversion to Saturnalia, with little awareness of its Christian meaning – though school nativity plays and church carol services are still remarkably popular.

Some Christians are so concerned about the overpowering mammon of the Christmas industry, and the way materialistic things now predominate, that they say (shades of the Puritans again!) they would rather celebrate the birth of Jesus on some other date. Yet, the two basic strands – the pagan midwinter festival and the celebration of the nativity – have been inextricably intertwined for so long that it seems better, if you are a Christian, to join wholeheartedly in the contemporary festival, making the most of the religious content which might otherwise be obscured or submerged.

Christians, in fact, can reclaim Christmas. Nor should they miss the many good things in this modern commercialized layer, such as the great boost to charitable giving by people of all faiths and none, the willingness to share with the poor and hungry, and the many encouraging indications of a compassionate and caring society.

So I invite you to taste this Christmas Trifle – not just the top, superficial layer, nor even just one of the layers beneath. If you want to have the very best Christmas, I believe you need to dig deep, spooning up something of everything, enjoying a delicious combination of flavours, textures – and aromas, for a richly traditional Christmas can be an aromatherapy in itself!

Christmas is not something we buy, but something we build. As Margo, in BBC TV's *The Good Life*, once said of Christmas: 'You can't have it delivered. You have to make it yourself.' And the more you put into it, the more you get out of it. The fairy-tale out-of-this-world atmosphere does not just happen. It has to be created. Customs can be revived, traditions maintained, and there are lots of things to read and think about in the following pages that can enhance your appreciation of Christmas and help to revive a festival that for many has lost its delight and become hollow and disappointing.

Many families have their own little traditions that make Christmas so special for them. Let me finally tell you a little more of our own. First, I find it important to go back to the roots, to read once again the Gospel accounts, however familiar, of the birth in Bethlehem. To add colour to this we think of our pilgrimage to the Shepherds' Field near Bethlehem, then how we stooped low to enter the Church of the Holy Nativity, and touched the silver star said to mark the very place where 'Mary bore sweet Jesus Christ'. I can even recall from long ago a visit to Cologne Cathedral to see the golden shrine supposed to contain the bones of the Wise Men. No need to travel, of course. Selective television viewing can bring us some memorable scenes, paintings and so forth, which will help to provide this kind of authentic Christmas imagery.

Music is another essential component of the Christmas atmosphere – the great works of Bach and Handel, for example, but especially the carols. And it's surely not enough to hear them, certainly not as background jingles in stores and supermarkets. You need to sing them for yourself, perhaps with others in church, and ideally in the open air, if you can join in the age-old custom of going carol singing in your neighbourhood.

Most important of all is what we do at home. I go to some trouble – as many people do – not only to set out the Christmas cards, decorate the Christmas tree, and put up the fairy lights, but also to add traditional decorations of holly and ivy, with a strategically suspended bunch of mistletoe, as well as candles, nativity light and an enlarged reproduction of the first Christmas card of 1843. Central to everything is the nativity scene, with its tiny hand-painted figures, which I made for our eldest daughter when she was a toddler. We have brought it out every Christmas since, giving it central place on top of the television set, to remind us of our priorities.

Thanks to my wife toiling away so expertly in the kitchen, we have all the customary Christmas dishes and delicacies, and include as many as possible of the traditional things you will find in this book. We've even served frumenty, and one year I reconstructed the finger-burning Victorian game of snapdragon. The family regards me as a Christmas fanatic, an eccentric and incorrigible romantic. Yet anything is better than spending Christmas passive and comatose, slumped in front of the phoney Christmas of non-stop TV.

We need something, as Dickens put it, 'to win us back to the delusions of our childhood days'! Young and old, let us rediscover and cherish our traditions. For example – not the artificial plastic sprig of mistletoe doing the rounds at some rowdy party for a promiscuous 'kiss me quick!' – but the real thing, taken seriously, with thoughts of its ancient origins and fabled powers adding a touch of romance.

With all the glitter and colour brought by electronic wizardry to our TV screens, what irony it is if we allow our Christmas to become a standardized, featureless thing of black and white! So read on ... and may you manage to achieve that wonderful feeling of solidarity with those who have gone before, the sense of being part of something that is both ancient and international, so much bigger than ourselves, bringing food for the starving millions, and peace, hope, comfort and refreshment to those who need it most. There really is nothing like Christmas – and may yours be a truly happy one!

Arnold Kellett
Knaresborough, North Yorkshire
October 2006

Abbot of Unreason The Scottish equivalent of the Lord of Misrule*, who took charge of the festivities during the Twelve Days of Christmas* in medieval times.

Abolition of Christmas The Puritan hostility to the keeping of Christmas resulted in its abolition by Act of Parliament in 1652. (See **Puritans**) In modern times the celebration of Christmas has been made illegal by certain repressive political regimes, and it is never observed by the sect of Jehovah's Witnesses, who claim that, as a festival, it has no scriptural warrant. In fiction, a classic television episode of *Porridge*, 'No Way Out', (1975), showed the officer, Mr Mackay, announcing that, because of a suspected planned escape, 'There will be no Christmas Eve, no Christmas Day*, no Boxing Day* – only the 24th, 25th and 26th of December.' In recent years certain politically-correct authorities have banned Christmas symbols and celebrations on the ground that these might possibly offend non-Christians. (See **Scrooge**)

Adeste Fideles (See **O come, all ye faithful**)

Adoration The term used to describe depictions in art of the visits to the Christ-child, namely the Adoration of the Shepherds (Luke 2.15-20) and the Adoration of the Magi (Matthew 2.11-12). (See **King's College Chapel**)

Advent The season which precedes Christmas and serves as a time of preparation for the celebration of the birth of Jesus*. In former times, and in some denominations still, it is also observed as a period of fasting as a prelude to the time of feasting. The name is derived from Latin *adventus* (arrival). Roman Catholics and Protestants observe four Sundays in Advent immediately before Christmas, but in the Eastern Orthodox Churches the season begins in mid-November.

Advent is regarded as the beginning of the church year, and its dual purpose is shown by the Anglican collect, repeated on each Sunday in Advent, which recalls not only the first coming of Christ ('in which thy Son came to visit us in great humility') but also anticipates the second coming or Second Advent ('in the Last Day, when he shall come again in his glorious Majesty to judge both the quick and the dead'.)

Bach's cantata *Wachet Auf!* ('Sleepers, awake!') was written to be performed on the First Sunday in Advent. Typical Advent hymns are 'O come, O come Emmanuel!' and 'Hark, the glad sound the Saviour comes'! (See **Stir-up-Sunday**)

Advent Calendar Christmas scenes on a cardboard sheet, with hinged perforations numbered from 1-24. The little doors are opened a day at a time, revealing a picture of some item connected with Christmas – a toy*, angel*, candle*, lantern, fruit* etc. The twenty-fourth door, opened on Christmas Eve, reveals the baby in the manger*. Advent calendars appear to have originated in Germany*, but are now popular amongst children* throughout the world, especially when they contain sweets, or other treats.

Advent Wreath The German custom of setting up an *Adventkranz* to herald the approach of Christmas has now been widely adopted by other countries, especially in churches. It is said to have been devised in 1833 by the Hamburg pastor, J.H. Wichern, who lit a series of candles* when he spoke about Christmas to the children* in his orphanage. The Advent wreath consists of five candle-holders arranged in the form of a cross in a circle decorated with evergreens*. On Advent Sunday one candle is lit, on the second Sunday in Advent, two candles – and so on, until by Christmas all four candles are burning, with an additional one for Christmas Day*. Various traditions give each of the four candles a particular association, a common one in British churches being (1) the people of God, (2) the Prophets, (3) John the Baptist (4) Mary the mother of Jesus. (See also **Wreaths**)

Advertising Although advertising is such a familiar aspect of the modern commercialized Christmas, and forces itself upon us mainly through print and television, it is not as recent as might be supposed. From at least the eighteenth century goods have been advertised by tradesmen, shops and stores, and it was once very common for workers such as night watchmen to hand out leaflets carrying an appeal in verse for a Christmas gratuity. A good example of how images are exploited by the Christmas industry is the use of Santa Claus by Coca-Cola. (See **Santa Claus**)

Albert, Prince Consort (1819-61) After his marriage to Queen Victoria* in 1840 Prince Albert, son of the Duke of Saxe-Coburg-Gothe, helped to introduce into England the German custom of setting up a decorated Christmas tree*. He first prepared such a tree for the Queen at Windsor Castle in 1841, and in 1848 there was a detailed description in the *Illustrated London News,* which carried a full-page engraving of a fully decorated tree being admired by Victoria, Albert and their children. This undoubtedly helped to popularize the use of Christmas trees in England, as did the large tree put up at Christmas 1854 on the site of the Great Exhibition of 1851, for which Albert was largely responsible. Prince Albert was also associated with the first Christmas card* in that he was a close friend of the organizer of the Great Exhibition, Henry Cole*, the man who in 1843 issued the first commercially-produced cards.

Alcohol (See **Drinks**)

Ale Posset A traditional West Country drink for Christmas Eve, consisting of hot, spiced ale mixed with milk and sugar.

All Heal Another name for mistletoe*, which from time immemorial has been believed to possess remarkable properties of healing. These were especially associated with the white berries and the sticky substance they exude, which does, in fact, contain compounds which in recent years have been used for the treatment of hypertension, cancer and other conditions. In ancient times mistletoe was believed to cure everything from toothache to epilepsy, and its very presence in the home was thought to have a therapeutic value.

Amahl and the Night Visitors A Christmas opera written for television by Gian Carlo Menotti. It was commissioned by the American NBC and first televised on Christmas Eve 1951, the composer having been inspired by memories of visits by the Three Kings during his Italian childhood, and also the Bosch painting of the *Adoration of the Magi*. It concerns a crippled shepherd boy who offers his crutch as a gift for the Magi to present to Jesus*, and is miraculously cured. *Amahl,* the first opera ever written for television, has received as many as 500 performances worldwide at Christmas-time.

Angel Angels play an important part in the story of the birth of Jesus*. The word is derived from the Greek for messenger, and according to St Luke's Gospel the first supernatural message announcing that Jesus would be born was brought to Mary* by the Angel Gabriel*, an event known as the annunciation* (Luke 1.26-38). According to St Matthew's Gospel 'the angel of the Lord' appeared to Joseph* in a dream, telling him not to be afraid to take Mary, already pregnant, as his wife, and adding that the baby must be named 'Jesus' (Matthew 1.18-23).

The best-known mention of an angel is in Luke's account of the sudden appearance to the shepherds* of the angel of the Lord, whose message – most familiar in the Authorized Version of the Bible – begins: 'Fear not, for behold, I bring you good tidings of great joy.' Immediately after announcing the birth of the Messiah* the angel is accompanied by a host of angelic beings singing the famous words, 'Glory to God in the highest, and on earth peace, good will toward men', also well-known in the Latin, beginning *'Gloria in excelsis'* (Luke 2.8-14). After the visit of the Wise Men* the angel of the Lord again appears to Joseph in a dream, warning him to flee with Mary and Jesus to Egypt in order to escape the wrath of Herod* (Matthew 2.13).

Angels are frequently mentioned in carols*, though perhaps the best-known line, 'Hark! The herald angels sing', was not what Charles Wesley originally wrote. (See **Hark! The herald angels sing**) From at least as early as Victorian times it has been traditional to place the figure of an angel at the very top of the Christmas tree*. The 1848 Christmas edition of the *Illustrated London News*, which popularized the royal tree at Windsor, included the comment: 'On the summit of the tree stands the small figure of an angel, with outstretched wings, holding in each hand a wreath.' As time went on the angel tended to be replaced by a winged doll or 'fairy doll'.

Belief in angels as spiritual beings occurs in several religions, including Islam, but there are 300 references to angelic beings in the Bible, and they are mainly associated with Christianity, where named angels, principally Michael, Gabriel and Raphael, can be prayed to. Non-Christian religions, especially in ancient Egypt*, Greece and Persia, have helped to form the image of angels, including their having wings. Though this is mentioned by Isaiah* and in Revelation, where angels are also described blowing trumpets. (See **Angel Chimes**)

Angel Chimes   A Christmas ornament, originating in Sweden, usually consisting of four angels* stamped out of thin brass plate and represented as blowing a trumpet. Three of them rotate, touching two small brass bells to produce a pleasant tinkling sound, while the fourth surmounting angel is carried round as they move. The motive power is the heat rising from four candles*, which also give the angel chimes an attractive appearance.

Angels from the realms of glory   A hymn, used as a carol*, written by the Moravian minister, James Montgomery, for his newspaper *The Sheffield Iris*. It appeared on Christmas Eve, 1816, and is based on the old French carol 'Les anges dans nos campagnes'.

Anglo-Saxons   A term used to describe the ancestors of the English, whose name is derived from the Angles, a race who tended to settle in the north and east, whereas the Saxons mainly settled in the south and west. The pagan Anglo-Saxons celebrated the revival of the sun after the winter solstice* with the festival of Yule-tide*, in a similar way to the Scandinavians*, whose gods such as Odin* they also shared, calling him Woden*. The change from the pagan Yuletide to Christmas was firmly established by Alfred the Great (849-99), who was a devout and scholarly Christian. He is said to have been the first to introduce the Twelve Days of Christmas* and *Christes Maesse* as a church festival, though tradition claims that Christmas was observed in England as early as 521, when the Celtic King Arthur is said to have attended a Christmas service in York Minster.

Several of the English Christmas customs can be traced back to the Anglo-Saxons, in particular the burning of yule-candles*, yule-logs* and the term wassailing*, which is derived from an Anglo-Saxon greeting.

Animals and other creatures Animals have an ancient association with Christmas, mainly because of St Luke's account of the nativity* which implies that the baby was born in a stable and states that Mary* travelled from Nazareth to Bethlehem* (nearly 80 miles) traditionally on a donkey.

Though there is no mention of it in Luke's Gospel there is an old idea that the shepherds* brought the gift of a lamb, sometimes shown in nativity scenes*, which also usually contain models of an ox and an ass, and sometimes a camel, associated with the Wise Men*. An actual ox and ass was used by St Francis* in his crib* of 1223. The tradition no doubt has its roots in the Old Testament prophecy: 'The ox knows its owner, and the ass his master's crib' (Isaiah 1.3).

There are many legends concerning animals and birds at Christmas. A broadsheet of 1631 depicts various creatures in the stable, uttering their characteristic cries in Latin: 'The Cocke croweth *Christus Natus est* (Christ is borne), the Raven asked *Quando?* (When?), the Crow replyed *Hac Nocte* (This Night), the Oxe cryed out *Ubi?* (Where?) The Sheepe bleated out *Bethlem.*'

Country districts used to retain the old belief that on Christmas Eve animals were endowed with the power of speech, that the sheep turned to face Bethlehem and that at midnight the oxen went down on their knees. This last belief was held as recently as the end of the nineteenth century in the West Country, shown in Thomas Hardy's poem, 'The Oxen', in which he imagines himself going to the stable on Christmas Eve, 'hoping it might be so'. One of the quaintest of old country beliefs is that bees can be heard buzzing the melody of the Old Hundredth in their hives at midnight on Christmas Eve.

The glow-worm, a flying beetle, is said to owe its light to having been touched by the Christ-child. Even the humble spider has a place in Christmas folklore, and is said to have woven a web over the entrance to the stable-cave to deter Herod's soldiers from finding the child. (See **Cock-crow, Herod, Robin, Tinsel, Wren**)

Annunciation The annunciation or, more simply, the announcement, was the message delivered to Mary* by the Angel Gabriel* that she was to be the mother of the Messiah* (Luke 1.26-38). Its words are familiar both in English ('Hail, thou that art highly favoured!' AV) and in Latin, especially in the form of the prayer or hymn, *Ave, Maria!* The annunciation is commemorated by the festival of Lady Day, on 25 March, and is referred to in many carols*, in

particular the beautiful Basque carol 'The Angel Gabriel from heaven came'.
(See **Basque Christmas**)

Apples Apples have a long association with Christmas, ranging from the apple which was sometimes placed in the mouth of the boar's head*, and the apple-sauce which invariably accompanies roast pork*, to the splendid red apple which, along with an orange* and a new penny, it is traditional to find in a Christmas stocking*. The Christmas apple should be bright red, like those which used to be distributed in Ripon Cathedral (See **Rosemary**). Their special use at this season may be explained by the Norse myths which tell of the gods eating apples to ensure immortality – the possible origin of the saying 'an apple a day keeps the doctor away'. Red apples were also symbolic of the sun. (See **Kissing Bough**) Roasted apples were an important ingredient of the wassail bowl as we know from many old recipes and descriptions such as that given by Charles Dickens* in *Pickwick Papers*. (See **Wassail Bowl**)

Apple Wassailing An ancient Christmas custom originating in prehistoric times, designed to ensure that the apple trees would bear a good crop. Originally common in the south and west of England it now survives mainly in a few parts of the West Country. As soon as it is dark – on a day usually around Twelfth Night* – the owner of the orchard leads a party to one of his best trees, where they pour cider round the roots, place a cake or toast soaked in cider and ginger on the tree and fire shotguns through the branches. They then sing a traditional apple-wassailing song such as:

> Here's to thee auld apple-tree,
> Whence thou may'st bud
> And when thou may'st blow
> And when thou mayest
>   bear apples enow,
> Hats full, caps full,
> Bushel, bushel sacks full,
> And my pockets full too! Huzzah!
> (See **Wassailing**)

Ashen Faggot The burning of the ashen faggot is a West Country equivalent of the burning of the yule-log*, still practised in parts of Somerset, Devon and Cornwall. A large bundle is made of green faggots from an ash – a tree which has ancient associations with witchcraft. The bundle is tightly bound with nine bands of ash, preferably from the same tree, or strips of hazel.

Ideally, the ashen faggot is lit from a remnant of the previous year's faggot, preserving the idea of continuity of life, as in the case of the yule-log. One tradition was for unmarried girls to choose a particular band. The girl whose band was the first to burst with the heat would be the first to marry. When the ashen faggot is burnt in an inn, the bursting of each band indicates that it is time for a round of cider, a custom still observed in the Luttrell Arms at Dunster, Somerset, where the faggot is lit at 7.00 a.m. every Christmas Eve.

Auld Lang Syne Traditionally sung while joining hands, to let in the new year, especially at Hogmanay*, this Scots dialect song by Robert Burns is about drinking in memory of *auld lang syne* (days long ago).

Australia Although the Australian Christmas is inevitably celebrated in hot and sunny weather, it retains many of the features brought by settlers from the northern hemisphere, including a minority who still feast on turkey* and Christmas pudding*. In addition to simulated northern evergreens* such as holly*, ivy* and mistletoe*, local plants are used for decoration, including the yellow-flowered Australian Christmas tree* (*Nuytsia floribunda*). Australia welcomes the arrival of Father Christmas*/Santa Claus* on the continent, where he lands on Bondi Beach, Sydney.

Australia adds to the traditional carols* some of its own, such as 'The Three Drovers', and originated the popular custom of open-air 'Carols by Candlelight', first organized by the radio presenter Norman Banks, in Alexandra Gardens, Melbourne in 1938. The most characteristic feature of the Australian Christmas, however, is the beach barbecue for family and friends.

Austria With its snow-capped mountains Austria has the ideal background for the celebration of Christmas, and is especially rich in tradition. The season opens with the visit of Saint Nicholas* on 6 December, when the costumed saint visits homes and schools and walks in procession, sometimes accompanied by the comic devil Krampus, who carries a rod or whip to punish naughty children. (See **Knecht Ruprecht, Père Fouettard**)

Christmas music is very important in Austria, which has given the world one of its best-loved carols. (See **Silent Night**) Catholic families announce the arrival of the Christ-child on Christmas Eve, when the story of the nativity* is read, and presents are opened. As well as a candlelit tree Austrian homes often display a crib* made by Tyrolean craftsmen. Festive food is similar to that in Germany*, with emphasis on a variety of spice-flavoured cakes and biscuits.

The Austrian equivalent of the Twelve Days of Christmas* is the period of *Rauhnächte*, when homes are traditionally purged of evil spirits by incense, and there are processions of masked figures. At Epiphany* the Three Kings go round the neighbourhood blessing houses, marking the doorposts with the date of their visit.

Ave Maria A Latin prayer based on the annunciation* of the birth of Jesus*, the message delivered to Mary* by the Angel Gabriel*. The English version

15

is 'Hail, Mary, full of grace, the Lord is with thee. Blessed art thou amongst women, and blessed is the fruit of thy womb, Jesus. Holy Mary, Mother of God, pray for us sinners, now and at the hour of our death. Amen.'

The Ave Maria is often sung as a hymn or religious song, especially at Christmas. The most familiar musical settings are those by Bach (arranged by Gounod) and by Schubert.

Away in a manger   A children's* hymn, now a popular carol*, sung in Britain to the tune by the American musician W.J. Kirkpatrick (1828-1921). The words appeared anonymously in 1885 in the USA in a collection of Lutheran hymns, but there is nothing to support the claim that the original was by Martin Luther*.

Baboushka   A female Christmas gift-bringer. (See **Russia**)

Baddeley Cake   A unique Twelfth Cake (See **Christmas Cake**) eaten every year at Drury Lane Theatre on Twelfth Night*, observed on 6 January. It is named after Robert Baddeley, a chef who became a very successful actor. On 19 November 1794 he was in his dressing room of the Theatre Royal, Drury Lane, preparing to take part in Sheridan's *School for Scandal,* when he collapsed and died. It was found that in his will he had left £100, the interest from which was to provide wine and a Twelfth Cake for the company acting at Drury Lane on every Twelfth Night. This provision has been taken very seriously, and ever since 1794 the actors in costume have met each year in the Green Room of the Theatre Royal, awaiting the arrival of the magnificent iced Baddeley Cake, ceremonially carried in by ushers dressed in eighteenth-century livery.

Balthazar   Traditional name of the third Wise Man, depicted in art as dark-skinned, sometimes associated with Ethiopia, holding the gift of myrrh*. (See **Wise Men**).

Bambino   The figure of the Christ-child in a crib*, especially in Italy*, from *bambino* (child). (See **Nativity Scene**)

Barring-out   The extinct custom of school-children locking out their teacher until a holiday was granted, sometimes done on St Nicholas's* Day (6 December).

Baubles   These probably started as an artificial reminiscence of the early tree decoration of apples*. (See **Paradise Tree**) The first hollow baubles of the thinnest coloured glass, known as *Kugeln* (spheres*), were made in Germany*, especially in the town of Lauscha, from 1867, and eventually sold by the million in Woolworth's department stores. (See **Wessle-Bob**)

Basque Christmas   The Basques of northern Spain* traditionally start their celebration when *Olentzero*, a figure in the guise of a shepherd or charcoal-burner, comes down from the mountains to distribute gifts. Some of the fine carols* in the unique Basque language have become well known, such as *'Birjinia gaztettotbat zegoen'* ('The Angel Gabriel from heaven came').

19

Bay A traditional Christmas decoration*, the use of which dates back to Roman* times, when bay leaves, also used to make 'wreaths of laurel' (an alternative name) were amongst the evergreens* used at the festival of Saturnalia*. Along with rosemary*, bay leaves were used in medieval England to make a garland for the boar's head*. One version of the Boar's Head Carol* includes the lines:

> The Boar's Head in hand bear I
> Bedecked with Bays and Rosemary.

Bay was used as a Christmas decoration well into the seventeenth century, and the leaves are still used to add flavour to various savoury dishes.

Bees (See **Animals and other creatures**)

Befana A female Christmas gift-bringer, said by the Italians to have been too busy to join the Wise Men*, which meant that she arrived in Bethlehem* too late to see the Christ-child. Ever since, she has wandered the earth, and at Epiphany* (*Epifania*, in Italian, of which her name, Befana, is a corruption) she brings gifts to children*. (See **Italy**)

Belgium Christmas in northern Belgium amongst Flemish-speakers has much in common with Holland, and in southern Belgium has largely French features. Traditionally shoes are left out to be filled with presents by St Nicholas*, but there is also a Christmas visit by *le Père Nöel* or *le Petit Jésus*. An interesting Belgian rejection of the usual self-indulgence of Christmas is the silent walk on Christmas Eve from Antwerp to Viesel, where worshippers have their feet washed by a priest and eat a simple meal of bread and cheese*.

Bellman The town crier, who traditionally rang his handbell* and recited verse to proclaim Christmas and beg gratuities, until the practice died out in the nineteenth century. (See **Waits**)

Bells The ringing of church bells has a long association with Christmas, but there is no historical evidence to indicate when they were first used to celebrate the birth of Christ*. There is a tradition that bells were introduced by Bishop Paulinus in about 420 AD, but the first clear mention of regular use is by St Gregory of Tours, who frequently refers to the ringing of church bells in France in about 585 AD.

In England some churches ring Christmas in with a peal of bells on St Thomas's* Day (21 December) and many similarly ring in the New Year*. The most interesting English custom connected with bell-ringing is performed every Christmas Eve at Dewsbury in Yorkshire, when the tenor bell of the parish church is tolled once for every year since the birth of Christ, a custom possibly dating from the thirteenth century. (See **Devil's Knell**) The most famous Christmas bells - broadcast all over the world on Christmas Day - are those which peal out from Bethlehem* from the Church of the Holy Nativity*, the oldest church in Christendom. (See also **Handbells**)

Bethlehem   Six miles south of Jerusalem, Bethlehem is situated in the fertile hill country of Judaea, which no doubt explains why its name is Hebrew for the 'House of Bread'. Bethlehem is associated with such famous Old Testament people as Rachel, Ruth and David, and is world famous as the birthplace of Jesus*. Although he is known to history as Jesus of Nazareth (the Galilean town where he grew up) we are told by St Luke how he came to be born in Bethlehem as the result of Joseph* returning there to his ancestral home, to be registered in a census ordered by Caesar Augustus*. (See **Nativity**). In St Matthew's account the emphasis is on the fact that the prophet Micah (5.2) had declared that the Messiah* would be born in Bethlehem, 'in royal David's city', as the carol* puts it.

Modern Bethlehem is still visited by vast numbers of pilgrims and tourists, who fill Manger Square and also visit the Shepherds' Field.* They come especially to see the ancient church built over what is traditionally supposed to be the actual birthplace of Jesus - a small cavern once used as a stable, probably originally underneath a house, built in the style which can still be seen in Bethlehem. Such a cavern is mentioned as the birthplace by Justin Martyr (100-167 AD) and was deliberately defiled by Hadrian (117-138 AD), though the first church there was not built until 330 AD after it had been visited by St Helena, the mother of the Emperor Constantine.

Other places named after Bethlehem are in Pennsylvania, USA, which has built a whole economy on the name, and also in South Africa and in a village in South Wales. (See **Church of the Holy Nativity**)

Birds   (See **Cock-crow, Robin, Wren**)

Bishop   A traditional hot drink of spiced wine, usually port*, referred to by Charles Dickens* in *A Christmas Carol*, when Scrooge* proposes to Bob Cratchit that they chat over 'a Christmas bowl of smoking (steaming) hot bishop'. (See **Mulled Wine**)

Blessing the Waters In the Greek Orthodox Church the ancient custom on 6 January of a priest throwing a cross into a river or the sea, to be retrieved by a diver. This rounds off the Christmas season and is said to drive away evil spirits.

Boar's Head The medieval ceremony of carrying in for the Lord's table a specially-decorated boar's head, to the accompaniment of the singing of a Boar's Head Carol*, is a traditional way of starting a Christmas feast. The practice dates from very early times and is particularly associated with the Scandinavian* veneration of pork* the food of the gods in Valhalla.

The most famous surviving boar's head ceremony takes place at Queen's College*, Oxford, where its survival from Tudor times or earlier is probably explained by the fact that students from the north of England often spent their Christmas in Oxford instead of making the long and difficult journey home. An implausible legend is that a student at Queen's was once confronted by a wild boar in Shotover Forest and that he killed it by thrusting a copy of Aristotle between its open jaws – hence the origin of the custom! At Queen's College the boar's head is carried into the hall by four servants, on a silver dish presented in 1668 by Joseph Williamson. The

procession is led by trumpeters, and choristers singing the famous Boar's Head Carol. They halt three times as the chief chorister sings one of the verses. When the high table is reached the Provost removes the orange* from the boar's mouth, and presents it to the chief chorister. He also removes some of the sprigs of evergreen* with which it is garlanded, and presents these to the principal guests.

The boar's head is attractively decorated with rosemary*, bay*, holly* and mistletoe*, and is traditionally served with mustard. At Hurstpierpoint College in Sussex, the choir is led by a boy carrying a pot of mustard, and at the end of the boar's head procession comes the cook with his carving knife and steel. Boar's head feasts still take place in various other colleges and schools, such as Ashville College in Harrogate, and by tradition the choirboys of St Paul's Cathedral sing at the feast of the Cutlers' Company of London.

Boar's Head Carol The carol* which is sung as the boar's head* is carried in procession into the dining-hall. The oldest version appears in the collection by Wynkyn de Worde (1521), but it is certainly from an earlier date, and was probably originally entirely in Latin. Versions now used are a mixture of Latin and English, for example:

> The Boar's Head in hand bear I ...
> *Caput apri defero,*
> *Reddens laudes Domino*
> (The Boar's Head I carry in,
> Giving praises to the Lord).

Boxing Day Made an official Bank Holiday in the UK in 1871, though not universally observed, Boxing Day is nevertheless an important part of the Christmas break in Britain and Commonwealth countries. There are two explanations of this name for the 26 December, which was originally called St Stephen's Day. (See **Feast of Stephen**) One explanation is that the day after Christmas it was customary to open the box (still seen in some churches) into which the congregation had put alms for the poor. As such charitable gifts would reach their maximum on Christmas Day*, the alms-box was opened the day after on St Stephen's Day, and the money distributed.

The other explanation is that the name originates from the custom of apprentices, tradesmen and servants carrying round a box, sometimes of earthenware, into which employers and customers were invited to place a gift of money. These were opened, or broken into pieces, on St Stephen's Day and the money either shared out or spent on a feast. An echo of this second custom can be heard in the term 'Christmas box', especially when it is used to describe a gratuity given for the past year's work, for example, to a newspaper boy.

It has become traditional to hold sporting events on Boxing Day, including fox-hunting which, in spite of government restrictions, still had meets, as many as 350, on Boxing Day 2005. Other activities range from football matches to the Boxing Day Tug of War across the River Nidd at Knaresborough, North Yorkshire, started in 1968. Boxing Day 2004 will long be remembered for the tsusami which devastated large areas of the Far East, and evoked a generous international response. (See **Charities**)

Boy Bishop A medieval custom which took place in schools, churches and monasteries on the Eve of St Nicholas* (5 December), when a choirboy was dressed up as a bishop, wearing all the vestments, such as cope and mitre. It appears to have combined homage to St Nicholas* with the pagan tradition of the Lord of Misrule*, when the roles of master and slave were reversed. The Boy Bishop was served by church dignitaries, provided a feast for the choristers, and enjoyed power, lavish entertainment and popularity until Holy Innocents Day* (26 December), when he preached a sermon and rode out to bless the people. The custom was abolished by Henry VIII in 1541, revived briefly during the reign of Mary Tudor in 1544, then abolished by Elizabeth I. It has occasionally been revived in modern times, as at Hereford Cathedral.

Brandy A spirit distilled from wine, which explains its original name of 'brandwine', probably from the Dutch *brandewign*, i.e. burnt or distilled wine. Brandy is particularly associated with Christmas through Christmas pudding* and the game of snapdragon*.

Brawn One of several pork* dishes served at Christmas, especially popular in Elizabethan times and still well-known to Victorians, this is cold, chopped meat taken from the pig's head and forepart and pressed into a mould.

Brussels Sprouts A standard accompaniment of roast turkey*, these are the buds produced by a variety of cabbage, known by this name since the eighteenth century.

Bûche de Noël The French equivalent of the yule-log*, originally a log of

oak or some other tree, which was ceremonially burnt. The term is now used for an edible representation of the log, made from a kind of Swiss roll. Covered with chocolate, marked to resemble bark, or cream to resemble snow, it can be regarded as a sort of French Christmas cake*. (See **France**)

Burning the Clavie (See **Hogmanay**)

Caesar Augustus (63 BC-14 AD) The Roman* Emperor at the time of the birth of Jesus*. Called Octavian, he was the great-nephew of Julius Caesar, the title *Augustus* (venerable) being given to him by the Senate. St Luke tells us that he issued a decree that everybody in the Empire should be registered for the purpose of taxation, and that this was the first census of its kind, held in Palestine when Quirinius* was governor of the province of Syria. So it was the decree of Caesar Augustus which meant that Joseph had to go with Mary* to his ancestral home of Bethlehem*. (See **Joseph**)

Calenigg A Welsh gift presented at Christmas and New Year*, consisting of an apple* or orange* on three stems as legs, decorated with nuts and small sprigs of evergreens* and with a little candle* on top. Said to be of Roman origin, the Calenigg is given to bring good luck for the coming year.

Canada The classic white Christmas of snow and ice is more of a possibility in Canada than in many northern countries, and there is additional atmosphere provided by the traditions of the early French settlers, particularly in the province of Quebec. There is also more observance of British Christmas traditions in Canada than in the USA, and contributions from Native American customs, including the old Huron Carol*.

Amongst French Canadian traditions are *La Guignolée,* when people collected for charity* during Advent*, Midnight Mass*, followed by the *Réveillon*,* and carols especially associated with Canada, such as *'D' où viens-tu bergère?'* (See **Stamps**)

Candles The inseparable association of Christmas with candles is explained partly by the pagan origins of the festival, when a light shining in the darkness of midwinter was a symbol of returning life, and partly by the Christian concept of Jesus* as the Light of the world (e.g. 'The light shineth in darkness,' John 1.5 AV). The two ideas were combined in the burning of yule-candles*, which were thought to bring great prosperity for the coming year if lit on Christmas Eve and allowed to burn through the night, and sometimes through the Twelve Days of Christmas*. (See also **Nativity Light**)

Historically the majority of candles have been made from animal fat, hence the name tallow-candles. Better quality, more expensive, candles were made from beeswax, which gave off a delicate perfume of honey. The bees* had to produce six or seven pounds of honey for each pound of beeswax. Candles made from paraffin wax are a comparatively recent introduction, and were first made commercially in 1857.

Candles carried in procession form an important part of several Christmas rituals, especially that connected with the Queen of Light* in Scandinavia*, when the Queen wears a crown of lighted candles. It was once customary, especially in Ireland, to place a lighted candle in the window on Christmas Eve in memory of the legend that the Christ-child was guided by such a light to a welcoming house.

Small candles are also used in the pretty angel chimes* associated with Sweden, and were extensively used to illuminate Christmas trees* until they were replaced by electric fairy lights. The commonest use of candles at Christmas, apart from during church services, such as 'Carols by Candlelight', is as a table decoration*, when their golden light helps to create an old-world romantic atmosphere. (See also **Candlemas**, **Christingle**, **Festival of Nine Lessons and Carols**)

Candle Auctions   The custom of auctioning land to be let in order to provide money for charity often took place on 21 December (St Thomas's Day*). The name candle auction comes from the practice of sticking a pin into a lighted candle and granting the land to the last person to bid before the pin falls out. The custom still survives in parts of Lincolnshire, for example, and at Hubberholme, Wharfedale at New Year.

Candlemas   The church festival held on 2 February to commemorate the purification of the Virgin Mary* and the presentation of the baby Jesus* in the Temple in Jerusalem. Here a devout man called Simeon took the baby Jesus in his arms, describing him as 'a light to lighten the Gentiles' – hence the custom of churches lighting candles* on this day to the accompaniment of the *Nunc Dimittis*, the opening words of the prayer of Simeon in Latin ('Now, Lord, you let your servant go in peace') (Luke 2.22-35).

It used to be considered extremely unlucky to leave Christmas decorations* up after Candlemas, and it was widely believed that such neglect would cause a death in the household during the year. An interesting ceremony of Cradle Rocking takes place on the Sunday nearest Candlemas at Blidworth in Nottinghamshire. The most recently baptized baby boy is presented to the vicar who rocks him in an old wooden cradle decorated with leaves and flowers, before returning him to the parents while the *Nunc Dimittis* is sung. The custom is believed to date from the thirteenth century, and though it lapsed after the Reformation it has been revived since 1923. By coincidence 2 February is observed in the USA as Groundhog Day. Groundhogs are American marmots, a species of rodent, and they are seen as indicators of the weather ahead according to when they come out of hibernation.

Candy Cane   (See **United States**)

Cards (see **Christmas Cards**)

Carols Derived from the Italian *carolare*, meaning 'to dance in a ring', carols were originally a form of singing and dancing* to express great joy. The earliest, sung in spring and at the winter solstice*, were probably linked with fertility rites. Their particular association with Christmas is said to date from the time when Francis of Assisi* set up his nativity scene* at Greccio in 1223, and used religious verse, set to folk tunes. Hymns celebrating the birth of Jesus* were already in existence at this date and had been sung at least since the second century, when Telesphorus, Bishop of Rome in 127 AD, refers to the singing of *'Gloria in excelsis'*, the 'Angels' hymn', the oldest carol of all. Such Christmas hymns were in Latin, usually Gregorian chants, sung by choir and clergy. The Franciscan friar, Jacopone da Todi, who died on Christmas Day 1306, popularized true carols, less formal songs with a Christmas theme, sung in everyday language.

The difference between a carol and a hymn can be seen by comparing, for example, 'The holly and the ivy'* with 'Hark! The herald angels sing'*. The first bears traces of an ancient pagan fertility cult, the second expresses a deep religious conviction about the incarnation*. However, so many traditional carols are also expressions of religious faith, and so many hymns are now sung by carol singers, that the distinction has become insignificant.

All European countries have traditional carols in their own languages, which have been sung every Christmas for many centuries. An interesting survival which shows the transition from Latin hymns to carols in the vernacular is *'In Dulci Jubilo'*, which is in English (originally German), with a Latin refrain. In England the earliest printed collection of carols appeared in 1521, made by Wynken de Worde, the assistant and successor to William Caxton, and from this date printing helped to standardize carols whose words had showed considerable variation.

Unfortunately the Puritans* partly succeeded in suppressing carols in the middle of the seventeenth century, and although they continued to be sung, by the early nineteenth century musicians were beginning to make collections in the fear that carols might otherwise die out (e.g. Davis Gilbert in 1822, William Sandys in 1833, and John Mason Neale in 1853). Fortunately, Queen Victoria's* reign, as well as introducing the Christmas tree* and Christmas cards*, also brought a renewed interest in carol singing, both by choirs and congregations in churches and chapels, and by parties of Waits*. A good example of the Victorian revival of carols is seen in the setting by William Cummings of Charles Wesley's eighteenth-century words 'Hark! The herald angels sing' to the splendid tune by Queen Victoria's favourite composer, Mendelssohn.

Today the tradition of carol singing in the open air is rare compared with the days when, well before the traditional starting time of St Thomas's Day* (21

December), young children* went from door to door in ones or twos, ending their brief selection with the old jingle beginning: 'We wish you a merry Christmas!', interrupted by a knock or ring at the door in the expectation of money. Larger groups – sometimes first-class choirs – still go carol singing for charity* and round hospitals, and brass and silver bands, especially from the Salvation Army, also play carols to raise money.

Amongst the oldest traditional carols are *'Angelus ad Virginem'* (fourteenth century, mentioned by Chaucer), 'Adam lay y-bounden' (fifteenth century), 'The holly and the ivy', *'In Dulce Jubilo'**('Good Christian men rejoice'), the 'Drum Carol', 'I saw three ships', 'God rest you merry, gentlemen'. Two of our oldest carols were originally in 'musicals' – mystery plays or pageants from the sixteenth century. They are the beautiful, sad lullaby of the Coventry Carol*, and the less familiar Cherry Tree Carol*. More recent, in approximate chronological order, are the following: (those with separate entries are indicated*)

'The first Nowell'*, 'O come, all ye faithful!'*, (translated from the Latin, *Adeste Fideles*), 'While shepherds watched'*, 'Hark! The herald angels sing', 'Christians, awake!'*, 'Once in royal David's city'*, 'Away in a manger'*, 'Good King Wenceslas'*, 'O little town of Bethlehem'*, 'It came upon the midnight clear', 'We Three Kings', 'In the bleak midwinter'*, the 'Cowboy Carol', the 'Calypso Carol', 'Little Donkey' etc.

Certain carols are associated with particular areas (e.g. the Sussex Carol*) and in South Yorkshire a number of local carols are regularly sung in pubs. (See **Pub Carols**) Foreign carols often sung in English-speaking countries include 'Stille Nacht', from Austria* (see **Silent Night**'), *'Vom Himmel hoch'*, (see **Luther**), and *'Es ist ein' Ros' entsprungen'* from Germany*, *'Il est né, le divin Enfant*'* (France*), 'The Angel Gabriel' (Basque*), 'Torches, Torches' (Spain*), 'Rocking' and 'The Cuckoo' (Czechoslovakia). Several English carols are set to foreign melodies – e.g. 'Ding dong merrily on high', and 'Angels, from the realms of glory', are both set to old French carol tunes. (See individual carols, **Annunciation, Festival of Nine Lessons, Songs, Wenceslas**)

Carols by candlelight (See **Australia**)

Caspar (See **Kaspar**)

Charities The obligation to give to the poor and needy at Christmas time is a tradition as old as Christmas itself, seen in the Middle Ages in generous donations of food and clothing by royalty, nobility and the monasteries, and later in bequests recorded on charity boards in parish churches, providing for food to be distributed to the poor, along with the opening of 'poor boxes'.

(See **Boxing Day**) The Victorian enthusiasm for charitable giving at Christmas owed much to the crusading influence of Charles Dickens*. Modern charitable organizations such as Oxfam, Save the Children, Christian Aid etc. receive most of their income at Christmas, partly through the sale of millions of charity cards. (See **Christmas Cards**) One of the more recent popular ways of giving has been to send out a literal Christmas box, a shoe-box filled with small presents, especially for children. Desperate people overseas have been helped at Christmas, for example, by Band Aid organized by Bob Geldof during the Ethiopian famine (1984), which raised £8 million (see **Songs**), and the appeal following the tsunami disaster of Boxing Day 2004, when, by the last of the Twelve Days of Christmas*, the UK alone had raised £200 million in private donations. An impetus for generosity towards the world's hungry and destitute is the perception that Jesus*, in his lowly birth, identified with the poor and needy.

Cheese An important traditional item on the Christmas table, especially in country districts, was a specially-chosen whole cheese, usually made locally. In Yorkshire, for example, it might be a Wensleydale, Swaledale or Cotherstone cheese, important because in Yorkshire it is customary to eat cheese with Christmas cake*. On Christmas Eve, before the cheese was cut, it was traditional here for the master of the house to carve a cross in the top.

In addition to the cheeses mentioned above, there are many other British varieties. Some of the most popular are Caerphilly, Cheddar, Cheshire, Derby, Double Gloucester, Lancashire, Red Leicester, Shropshire Blue, White Stilton and Blue Stilton.

Cherry Tree Carol One of our oldest carols, this tells the legend of how Joseph*, angry to discover that Mary* is pregnant, refuses to pick cherries for her, but is amazed to see the cherry tree bend down so she can reach them. It is of interest also because it contains the tradition of Joseph's seniority, beginning:

> Now Joseph was an old man
> An old man was he,
> When he courted Virgin Mary,
> The Queen of Galilee.

Chestnuts Chestnuts have a long association with Christmas, when they are roasted on or by the fire, as mentioned by Charles Dickens*. They are also used to make chestnut stuffing for the turkey*, and candied as *marrons glacés**. (See **France**)

Childermas (See **Holy Innocents**)

Children Christmas is generally regarded as a child-centred festival, with its focus on the baby in the manger and the patron saint of children, St Nicholas* or Santa Claus*. Countless testimonies to happy childhood experiences at Christmas are recorded in diaries, letters and literature – for example, in *A Child's Christmas in Wales* (1954) by Dylan Thomas. Although the Christmas industry now encourages adults to spend as much as possible on themselves, the emphasis is still on toys and presents for children, increasingly expensive and sophisticated in contrast to the simple toys of earlier years. (See **Christmas Stocking, Nativity Plays, Toys and Games**)

China Christmas has infiltrated even the vast Peoples' Republic of China, especially in the cities, where there is a festive atmosphere in the stores, presided over by the Chinese equivalent of Santa Claus*, *Dun Che Lao Ren* ('Old Man Christmas'). Many Chinese people now exchange Christmas cards* and presents, but in this communist country only a small minority of Christians celebrate the birth of Christ, notably at overcrowded services in churches and the two cathedrals of Beijing. Some Christmas services are so popular that admission is by ticket only. As well as images such as nativity scenes, churches often set up a Christmas tree* hung with red envelopes containing money, the kind given at the Chinese New Year*. This money, however, is not distributed as personal presents, but given to charity*. The new 'Regulations on Religious Affairs' issued by the government in 2005 ensure that Christians have freedom to worship and celebrate Christmas, provided they do not use any compulsion or allow foreign interference.

Christ The title given to Jesus, meaning 'the one who is anointed' (i.e. by God). It is from the Greek word *christos*, which is a translation of the Hebrew word *Messiah** (the Anointed One). Anointing, the placing of holy oil on the head, was for the Hebrews the mark of royalty, and the Messiah was the one whom Old Testament prophets foresaw as being divinely commissioned to save the people. (See, especially, **Isaiah**) In the New Testament the title is given to Jesus by the angel*, particularly in the words 'To you is born this day... a Saviour, who is the Messiah, the Lord' (Luke 2.11).

Note that the name 'Jesus Christ' is not a forename and surname, like 'John Smith', but a title – more correctly 'Jesus the Christ' (or Messiah). The word eventually was transferred to the followers of the Christ, who were first called 'Christians' at Antioch in about 40 AD (Acts 11.26), and also to Christmas and Xmas*, the latter word preserving the original 'CH' of the Greek.

Christians, awake! The words of this Christmas hymn were written for Christmas Day* 1745, and given as a present to his daughter, Dolly, by John Byrom, a friend of John and Charles Wesley. Dr Byrom of Manchester was a scholarly physician who invented one of the earliest systems of shorthand.

His words are sung to the tune 'Yorkshire' (originally called 'Stockport'), composed by John Wainwright, organist of Manchester Parish Church. Byrom recorded in his diary that Wainwright and the Manchester choirboys came and sang the hymn outside his home at Christmas 1750. It is still sung to usher in many a Christmas morning, ideally at midnight on Christmas Eve by open-air carol singers.

Christingle A custom originating amongst the Moravian Brethren (founded by Count Zinzendorf* in 1722) and recently adopted by the Church of England Society for their annual Christingle Service held around Christmas. The first service of Christingle, derived from German *Christkind(lein)* (little Christ-child), was held in Marienborn on Christmas Eve 1747, when children* were given a candle tied with a red ribbon and asked to light it and place it in a window at home. During the picturesque service today each child receives a Christingle

which consists of an orange* (representing the world) stuck through with skewers on which are dried fruits* (representing the fruits of the earth) and tied with a red ribbon (representing the blood of Jesus*). A candle* is inserted into the top of the orange, representing Christ* as the Light of the world. During the singing of the Christingle hymn, 'Morning Star', the lights are extinguished and the church is illuminated by the candles. Although now associated with the raising of money for charity*, the origin of the Christingle was the Moravian zeal for missionary work and concern to preach the gospel throughout the world.

Christmas The celebration of the birth of Christ* is a Christian festival – originally Anglo-Saxon* *Cristes maesse*, or Christ's Mass – which has been kept since the early days of the Church, when it gradually replaced the Roman midwinter festival of Saturnalia* and later the Anglo-Saxon and Scandinavian* festival of Yule-tide*. As the Gospel accounts of the nativity* do not mention the day when Jesus* was born the early Christians made use of the most popular of the official Roman* holidays. During periods of persecution Saturnalia would be one of the few times when Christians could celebrate without being arrested, tortured and killed for making a public declaration of their faith.

Tertullian, around 200 AD, had objected to the way his fellow-Christians were celebrating like the pagans by lighting candles* and decorating their doors with evergreens*. But once Christianity was officially tolerated, then adopted, after Constantine became Emperor in 312 AD, Christians began to make full use of the Saturnalian festival, keeping the 25 December as Christmas Day. This had once been sacred to the Roman god Mithras, but now it was regarded as the day when Jesus was born, though Christians really celebrate it as the 'official' birthday, the actual date of the birth being unknown. (See **Christmas Day**)

As well as adopting Saturnalia, the early Christians also adopted and adapted some of its traditions, such as the use of holly*, which they now invested with Christian symbolism. As time went on Christmas absorbed customs from other ceremonies and festivals connected with the winter solstice* (see **Druids, Mistletoe, Yule-tide**, etc.) and became a unique blend of pagan and Christian tradition, with official endorsement, in particular from Gregory the Great*. On the one hand it retains primitive elements, much older than Saturnalia, connected with the fire rituals once used to revive the dying sun. On the other hand Christmas contains the profound theology of the incarnation, with carols* celebrating the gospel message that Jesus was nothing less than the eternal Word as flesh and blood. (See **Incarnation**)

However, the pagan elements – never much below the surface – dominated to such an extent that in the seventeenth century the Puritans* officially abolished Christmas, even outlawing it by a special Act of Parliament in 1652. With the Restoration of Charles II, the festival flourished once more, and in the nineteenth century was given additional charm and an even more romantic atmosphere by the Victorians, to whom we owe the introduction into England of the Christmas tree*, Christmas cards*, and the idea that Christmas is essentially a time for family reunions and charitable work. (See **A Christmas Carol, Dickens, Pickwick Papers** etc.)

In the twentieth and twenty-first centuries the mass production of a wide variety of traditional Christmas items, as well as every conceivable kind of Christmas present, has led to the season being commercially exploited on a staggering scale, and it is now a major industry, even in non-Christian countries, such as Japan*. As well as becoming grossly materialistic, Christmas is in danger of losing some of its ancient and picturesque customs, mainly through television, which now provides a focal point of Christmas entertainment, in place of the earlier family gatherings round the piano or by the fireside. However, the recognition that Christmas is a religious festival still survives in the well-attended school nativity plays*, carol services, Midnight Mass* (or Communion) on Christmas Eve and Christmas Day services, and especially in the countless carols which proclaim the 'good tidings of great joy'.

Christmas Archives   Launched in 1978 by Countess Maria Hubert von Staufer and her husband Andrew, a Polish Count, this is a reference library and research centre available on the internet. In 1991 they sold most of their huge collection of artefacts, including 40,000 Christmas cards*, to a Japanese company, providing the basis of a Christmas museum, later set up in Hakodate in the north of Japan.

Christmas Box   Though this term is now used for any Christmas present it originally referred to an actual box in which alms were collected. (See **Boxing Day**)

Christmas Cactus   (See **Zygocactus**)

Christmas Cake   The Christmas cake as it is known today had its origin in the Twelfth Cake which was served on Twelfth Night. Sometimes it contained a dried bean, and the person who found this in his slice was elected king or queen to preside over the party. (See **Epiphany, Twelfth Night, France**) Although this custom had largely died out by early Victorian times, the Twelfth Cake continued to be made, and pastry cooks vied with each other to produce lavishly iced fruitcakes, decorated with flowers, stars, crowns and figures of the Three Kings, whose visit occurred at Epiphany (See **Wise Men**). The Twelfth Night cake survives now only in the Baddeley Cake* of the Drury Lane Theatre, but although the present-day Christmas cake is not usually linked with any special ceremony, in many homes it is made well in advance of Christmas according to a recipe which may have been used by the family for several generations. (See also **Marzipan**). In the north of England, especially in Yorkshire, it is traditional to eat cheese with Christmas cake, locally known as 'spice* cake', providing a delicious contrast between the sharp tang of the cheese* and the rich sweetness of the cake.

Christmas Cards   Though now an essential part of Christmas, and universal in their use, Christmas cards did not appear until 1843 in Victorian England. Before this date it was not unusual to send Christmas greetings in the form of a letter, sometimes in verse, and in the eighteenth and early nineteenth centuries schoolchildren were encouraged to write a 'Christmas piece', displaying their copperplate writing for the gratification of their parents. The true Christmas card did not appear, however, until the practical Victorians devised this cheap and easy means of communication.

The artist William Dobson was possibly the first to send Christmas pictures, but it now seems clear that it was one of Dobson's artist friends, a young man who later became a Royal Academician, John Calcott Horsley*, who designed the first actual Christmas card, in 1843. This was at the request of Henry Cole*, later Sir Henry Cole, founder of the Victoria and Albert

Museum and a friend of Prince Albert*. It is said that this busy man forgot to send his usual Christmas greetings to his wide circle of friends and acquaintances, so he asked Horsley to design a card which could be mechanically reproduced, requiring only a signature. The claim that the artist W.M. Egley designed the first card is now usually discounted. The date is very indistinct, and the design is more elaborate than Horsley's, suggesting a development of his idea.

J.C. Horsley's card, which is a hand-tinted lithograph in attractive pastel shades, depicts a typical Victorian family who have completed their Christmas dinner and are now raising their glasses in a toast to absent friends. The picture also shows children* drinking wine, to which the temperance societies of the day objected. In the side panels, which are enclosed in trellis work entwined with greenery, are scenes showing food being given to the hungry and warm clothes being provided for the ragged poor. It bears the words 'A Merry Christmas and a Happy New Year to You'. A single copy exists signed by the artist himself, who had sent it 'to his *old* young friends, Emma and Agnes,' signing it *'J.C. Horsley, Xmasse 1843'*.

A thousand copies of this first lithographed card were printed by Jobbins of Holborn. When Cole and Horsley had taken what they needed the rest were sold at a shilling (5p) each at Summerly's Treasure House, a shop in Old Bond Street, owned by Cole. The idea quickly caught on and, as in the case of the Christmas tree*, was encouraged by royal example, Queen Victoria* herself sending 56 cards in 1847. The spread of the custom was further helped by the existence of the Penny Post (started in 1840, partly at Cole's suggestion) and the new half-penny rate for cards, introduced in 1870.

Cards were printed in colour from about 1868. Just before Christmas 1871 one newspaper editor made the surprisingly modern remark that people were 'trying to outdo one another in the number of cards acquired' and complained of 'the subsequent delay to legitimate correspondence'. By late Victorian times there were all kinds of elaborate cards, expensive, showy and sentimental, even in velvet and ivory and incorporating jewels. In the United States* black and white cards were printed by R.H. Pease in the 1850s, and in 1875 Louis Prang started issuing his popular cards in full colour.

The present flourishing industry in the UK, which produces untold millions of Christmas cards – usually about a year before they are actually sold – owes much of its impetus to Adolph Tuck, son of Raphael Tuck, who in 1880 organized a nationwide competition for the best card designs in Britain, offering 500 guineas in prize money. There were 5,000 entries, and the enterprising Mr Tuck even invited Tennyson to write verses for him, though the ailing Poet Laureate, then in his eighties, gracefully declined. It was in this same year, 1880, that the Post Office first issued the well-known appeal 'Post early for Christmas'.

36

The most striking development in Christmas cards is the evolution in their design – from the Victorian fondness for depictions of children, family gatherings, log fires, snow scenes, robins, stagecoaches, flowers, fruit*, butterflies etc. to a wide variety of contemporary images, including specifically Christian scenes and symbolism. One of the most successful firms was started by an 18-year-old American, J.C. Hall, and his two brothers in Kansas City in 1910. In 1928 they started using their trade name of 'Hallmark', which now has around 2,000 different designs.

Though only about a fifth of cards refer in any way to the birth of Jesus*, a third are charity cards. The first of these were devised in 1912 by Dr Wilfred Grenfell to raise money for his missionary work in Labrador and Newfoundland. In 1949 UNICEF launched a charity card designed by a seven-year-old Czech girl, Jitka Samkova. Cards posted in the UK alone now number around 750 million, in the USA around three billion. Although the exchange of cards has become almost automatic – a kind of signed receipt to show we are still living – they nevertheless contribute both to a sense of social cohesion and making Christmas colourful. (See **Charities, Cole, Robin, Round Robin**)

A Christmas Carol   The powerful story by Charles Dickens, *A Christmas Carol,* was written in a burst of inspiration within a few weeks, and published in December 1843 at the same time as the first known Christmas card*. Dickens's motivation was to raise money to support his wife and his first four children*, and also to make a protest about the gap between rich and poor. As no publisher would accept it, because it seemed too short for a book, Dickens paid for the printing himself, selling the 6,000 copies of the first print in a few days, but making little profit because it was pirated. However, he later used it for the highly popular public readings he gave for charity*.

This was one of the most influential books of the Victorian era, and did much to encourage the keeping of Christmas, not only as a merry festival, but as a time of kindness to the poor and needy. Its message is summed up by the view taken by Scrooge's nephew, who saw Christmas as 'a good time, a kind, forgiving, charitable, pleasant time; the only time I know of, in the long calendar of the year, when men and women seem by one consent to open their shut-up hearts freely, and to think of people below them as if they really were fellow-

travellers to the grave, and not another race of creatures bound on other journeys'. Several film versions have been made of *A Christmas Carol,* the first in 1901. One of the most popular was made in 1951, with an outstanding performance as Scrooge by Alastair Sim. (See **Dickens, Scrooge, Tiny Tim, Carols**)

Christmas Cherry A pot-plant belonging to the tomato family, the Winter or Christmas Cherry (*Solanum capsicastrum*) has conspicuous and long-lasting scarlet berries.

Christmas Crackers An indispensable decoration* on the Christmas table, dating from Victorian times, crackers consist of a brightly-coloured paper and a cardboard container designed to be pulled apart by two people. The crack is caused by the frictional rupture of two strips, glued together, enclosing a tiny amount of explosive, known in the trade as the 'snap'. The cracker usually contains a folded paper hat, motto or conundrum, and some trinket or puzzle.

Christmas crackers are believed to have been invented during the 1840s. It is said that a London confectioner, Tom Smith, first got the idea on a visit to Paris. Noticing the way the French sold *bonbons* of sugared almonds wrapped in a twist of paper, he marketed his own version in England, later adding a motto, mock jewellery and so on. Finally, influenced by Chinese firecrackers, and also the crackle from a log burning in his fireplace, he experimented with devising the well-known detonation. Though Tom Smith was the major developer of crackers, it is not clear that he actually invented them, because part of his firm's archives were lost when the building was damaged in an air raid in 1941. The company he founded dates from 1847, yet the use of the term 'cracker bon-bon' was recorded as early as 1841, and one is shown being pulled in the *Illustrated London News* in 1847, without any reference to Tom Smith.

Nicknamed *cosaques*, probably because they made a sound like Russian* Cossack riders cracking their whips, the new crackers became immensely popular, and had more varied and sometimes luxuriously expensive contents. By 1900 Tom Smith and Co. were selling 13 million crackers at Christmas, in more than a hundred bright designs, and in 1910 received from George V their first royal warrant.

Christmas Day The most important part of the festival of Christmas is the actual day (25 December, for Catholics and Protestants), when, as the carol* exhorts, 'Christians, awake! Salute the happy morn whereon the Saviour of the world was born'. Yet there is no mention of a date either in the New Testament or in any early non-Christian writing. All we are told is that Jesus* was born during a census ordered by Caesar Augustus*, when Quirinius* was governor of Syria (Luke 2.1) and Herod* the Great the ruler of Judaea (Matthew 2.1). Since Herod is known to have died in 4 BC, no more than two years after the nativity*, it is likely that the birth of Jesus took place around 6 BC. (Because of a miscalculation when the first Christian calendar was devised our dates AD are always at least six years out.)

As to the time of the year, it has been argued that the case for December is not very strong because the sheep were out in the open fields, unlikely in the Palestinian winter. However, western Christendom eventually adopted the 25 December, which had been the *Dies Natalis Solis Invicti* (the Birthday of the Unconquered Sun), the high point of the Roman midwinter holiday. (See **Saturnalia**) Tradition ascribes this change to a Bishop of Rome named Telesphorus, who died in 137 AD, but the first historical mention of Christmas Day does not appear until 336 AD, when the 25 December is described as *natus Christus in Bethlehem Judeae*. The date was not officially declared to be Christmas Day until the reign of Pope Julius I (337-52 AD).

When the old Julian calendar (named after Julius Caesar) was abandoned in favour of the more accurate Gregorian one, the Eastern Orthodox Church still kept the festivals as in the Julian calendar, so that some Christians, such as the Armenians, celebrate the birth of Jesus on 6 January (Epiphany* or Old Christmas Day*), and others, such as Russian*, Ukrainian and Coptic Christians, on 7 January.

Christmas Day has often been used for ceremonial occasions. In 597 AD, for example, many thousands of converts, including King Ethelbert, were baptized on Christmas Day as a result of St Augustine's mission to England. In 1066 William the Conqueror was crowned in Westminster Abbey on Christmas Day.

Christmas Day Broadcasts The first of these was made on radio by George V in 1932, following much persuasion by Lord Reith, Chairman of the BBC. Apparently written by Rudyard Kipling, the opening words of the speech were: 'Through the marvels of modern science I am enabled this Christmas Day to speak to all my peoples throughout the Empire.' The tradition was continued by George VI, who had to overcome a bad stammer, and who is best remembered for his speech on Christmas Day 1939, at the outbreak of war, when he quoted the poem by Minnie Louise Haskins beginning: 'I said to the man who stood at the Gate of the Year...'. His daughter, Elizabeth II, took over in 1952, first giving her speech on television on Christmas Day* 1957. (See **Queen**)

Christmas Day in the Workhouse This phrase is from the first line of a long poem 'In the Workhouse, Christmas Day,' by the Victorian journalist George R. Sims. The opening words are far better known than the poem itself, in which a poor widower bitterly denounces the workhouse guardians for allowing his wife to starve to death on the previous Christmas Day. It begins:

> It is Christmas Day in the Workhouse
> And the cold, bare walls are bright,
> With garlands of green and holly
> And the place is a pleasant sight
> For, with clean washed hands and faces
> In a long and hungry line,
> The paupers sit at the tables,
> For this is the hour they dine.

Christmas Island There are two islands of this name, one in the Indian Ocean, discovered by the English at Christmas in 1643; the other is in the Pacific Ocean, discovered on Christmas Eve 1777 by Captain Cook. There is also a lesser-known Christmas Island in Nova Scotia.

Christmas Oratorio J.S. Bach's set of six joyous cantatas, composed in 1734, designed to be played from Christmas Day* to Epiphany*.

Christmas Pie The term is known mainly through the curious old verse about Jack Horner 'eating his Christmas Pie'. Although he 'plucked out a plum' (the word once used for prunes or dried plums, and later for raisins) such pies were mainly of meat or poultry, with fruit* and spices* added. (See **Mince Pies**)

The most popular kind were Yorkshire Christmas Pies, containing a rich assortment of boned poultry, the larger birds enclosing smaller ones. In a recipe of Hannah Glasse (1747) a pigeon was placed inside a partridge, this inside a chicken, this inside a goose*, the whole enclosed by a turkey*, with

 woodcock and other game placed round it. These pies were made with strong, elaborately-decorated crusts, packed in boxes and sent from Yorkshire all over the country, especially to London. Still popular at Christmas are pork pies known as 'stand pies', so called because they are not served in a dish, but with crust firm enough for the pie to stand on its own. (See **Jack Horner**)

Christmas Pudding Although one of the most familiar of Christmas desserts, Christmas pudding in its present form only dates from about 1670. Before this it was a hot semi-liquid served at the beginning of the meal, and

known as plum porridge or plum pottage, similar to frumenty*. As in the case of mince pies* the original mixture was based on meat. Beef and mutton was stewed with dried fruit*, then the mixture was flavoured with wine, spiced with cloves, mace, ginger etc. and stiffened with breadcrumbs. In succeeding years the plum porridge tended to be made stiffer and stiffer until it evolved into its present form of solid pudding. The alternative name plum pudding* refers to the 'plums' (prunes or raisins) in the original plum porridge. The only link with the early meat content is the suet included in many recipes, but the other ingredients – flour, sugar, butter, eggs, currants, raising agent, sultanas, candied peel, mixed spice* etc. – have been used for centuries. A splendid plum pudding was made for George I, 'the Pudding King', at his first Christmas dinner in England in 1714. The largest ever made is said to have been for the community of Paignton, Devon, in 1819, which weighed 900 pounds.

Traditionally each member of the family is supposed to take a turn at stirring the mixture, making a secret wish. The Sunday before St Andrew's Day (30 November) was supposed to be the most propitious day for making the pudding. (See **Stir-up Sunday**)

Surviving customs include the placing of a small coin in the pudding mixture, supposed to bring good fortune to the person who finds it in his or her portion. A ring similarly found denotes a marriage, a thimble or button a single life. Dickens* tells us in *A Christmas Carol** (1843) that the pudding was steamed in the kitchen copper, then 'Mrs Cratchit entered – flushed, but smiling proudly – with the pudding, like a speckled cannon-ball, so hard and firm, blazing in half a quartern of ignited brandy*... with Christmas holly stuck into the top'. This custom is still observed in many homes, and brandy may also be served with the pudding in the form of brandy sauce or brandy butter.

Christmas Rose The white flower known as the Christmas Rose is not a rose but a member of the Hellebore family, related to the common buttercup, and its juice is poisonous. The Christmas Rose, *Hellerborus niger,* produces its low-growing but attractive flowers between December and February, and is often seen in bloom at Christmas.

Christmas Stocking The well-established custom of children* hanging up a stocking on Christmas Eve, in the expectation that it will be filled with toys and presents by Santa Claus*, appears to be connected with a story concerning the original Santa Claus, St Nicholas*. The saint had a reputation for doing good by stealth, leaving gifts for the poor in secret. One night he is said to have gone to the humble cottage of a man whose wife had died and who was so desperately poor that he was being forced to sell his three young daughters as slaves or prostitutes. On three successive nights Nicholas threw into the house some money which saved the girls from a life of degradation. One version of the story says he threw the money through the open door

(or window) but the more attractive version is that he climbed on the roof, dropped the money down the chimney, and it fell into the stockings the girls had left hanging in the fireplace to dry. Another variant is that the money fell into the girls' shoes, which accounts for the custom in France*, for example, of children leaving out shoes to be filled with presents.

As to what the money consisted of, there are two traditions. One says that it was three small bags of gold, possibly the origin of the little filigree bags of chocolate pennies covered in gold foil which are placed in Christmas stockings today. The other tradition is that it was three golden coins, the origin of the three golden balls used as a sign by pawnbrokers (who have St Nicholas as their patron saint) and also the origin of the old custom of placing in the stocking – along with an apple* and an orange* – a 'new penny'. There are accounts of stocking-filling in America by such writers as Clement C. Moore (1823) and Susan Warner, in her influential story, The Christmas Stocking (1854). The Christmas stocking was originally hung by the fireplace, but is now more commonly placed at the foot of the bed, along with a pillowcase for bigger presents, as shown in a silent film of Santa's visit made in 1890.

Christmas Tree The setting up of a decorated evergreen* tree – nowadays in Britain usually a small rooted Norwegian spruce fir or the topmost part of a young spruce – was almost unknown outside Germany* until the second half of the nineteenth century, when it became popular in England and the USA*. The use of all kinds of evergreens, including trees, as a symbol of continuing life is very ancient, and was known to both the Romans* and Scandinavians*. However, the special place of the *Tannenbaum* (fir-tree) in Germany, probably dates back to the eighth century when the English missionary Wynfrith, later known as St Boniface, felled an oak tree sacred to the old pagan god Thor, to whom a child was about to be sacrificed. Legend says that when Boniface had felled the oak he noticed a fir sapling growing between its roots. He is said to have told his Christian converts to regard this evergreen tree as a symbol of eternal life, and named it the tree of the Christ-child.

In the Middle Ages a fir-tree was always used as the *Paradiesbaum* (Paradise Tree) in German mystery plays*, hung with apples and surrounded by candles. The association of a decorated tree with Christmas has been attributed to Martin Luther*, who is said to have noticed the stars shining through the branches of a fir-tree as he returned home one Christmas Eve. According to pious legend, Luther pulled up a small sapling and decorated it with candles in imitation of the stars, with a candle at the top as a reminder of the Star of Bethlehem*. By the sixteenth century, in Luther's lifetime, there are references to evergreen trees in German homes at Christmas.

A description of Christmas trees at Strasbourg in 1605 tells us that they were decorated with roses cut out of multicoloured paper, flowers, apples*, beads, gingerbreads and other sweets. The custom spread to America, taken there by German settlers and soldiers from Hesse serving in the army, and it is mentioned as early as 1776 in Pennsylvania. The custom took longer to catch on in England. Although it was introduced by German merchants, especially in the Manchester area, it took royal precedent to make it popular. The first definite mention of a royal Christmas tree in England was in 1800, when Queen Charlotte, wife of George III, had a tree festooned with toys and sweets for children invited to Windsor Castle on Christmas Day. Other trees are mentioned at Windsor in 1821 and 1829.

However, it was not until Queen Victoria* married Prince Albert* that the Christmas tree became an essential part of the English Christmas. The Prince, a stickler for tradition, decorated a tree in his native German fashion at the Christmas spent at Windsor Castle in 1841. By 1848 the custom was such a well-established a part of the royal Christmas that an article on it appeared in the *Illustrated London News* with a full-page illustration, depicting a 'young fir about eight feet high', with six tiers of branches, on each of which were a dozen wax candles* and trays and eggs filled with sweets, fancy cakes, gilt ginger-bread etc. 'suspended by variously-coloured ribbons'. The tree is shown on a table covered with white damask, and underneath it are piles of larger sweets and 'toys and dolls of all descriptions'.

The publicity given to the Queen's tree at Windsor, personally prepared for her and their children by her husband, had the effect of spreading the custom throughout the country, so that soon it had been adopted almost everywhere. In 1850 Charles Dickens* was able to refer to that 'pretty German toy, the Christmas Tree', reminding us of its origins.

The largest trees were set up in public places: in 1854, for example, on the site of the Great Exhibition, another site associated with Prince Albert. The first electric fairy lights (much less a fire hazard than candles) appeared in about 1890. In 1909 a large illuminated tree was set up on Mount Wilson at Pasadena, California, from where the idea spread across the USA*, and from 1912 there has been a famous tree in Madison Square Gardens, New York. There is also one each year in front of the White House, whose lights are turned on by the President. The best-known public Christmas trees in England are the two presented by the Queen* to St Paul's Cathedral, and the huge illuminated tree in Trafalgar Square, the annual gift to the people of London from the people of Oslo, which first appeared in 1947 as a token of Norway's bond with Britain during the Second World War. The Norwegian spruce is usually up to 70 feet tall, with 650 lights.

Christmas trees, whether the still-popular real trees (some rooted) or the various realistic artificial kinds, are traditionally dismantled after Twelfth Night*, when children since at least Victorian times have been allowed to take the sweet and chocolate decorations as a recompense for helping. (See also **Angel**)

Christmas Truce A remarkable occurrence during the First World War at Christmas, 1914, when the fighting stopped spontaneously along much of the 600-mile Western Front. It started on Christmas Eve, when British troops heard the singing of 'Silent Night'* coming from the German* trenches. Soon they joined in, also singing other carols*. On Christmas morning they exchanged greetings shouted across no man's land, and some Germans came forward holding small Christmas trees* decorated with lighted candles*. Soon both sides left the mud of the trenches and ventured out into the open, shaking hands, talking to each other, showing family photos and exchanging little gifts such as their brass buttons, cigarettes, English bully-beef and German sausages.

They took the opportunity of this little unofficial armistice to bury the dead lying on the battlefield, and later even had friendly games of football. The truce lingered on through Boxing Day, but on strict orders from an outraged high command all fraternization was forbidden, discipline was restored and the shooting and shelling was resumed. The new year of 1915 was one of appalling losses, and was when the Germans started the use of poison gas. The truce was depicted on stage in *Oh, What a Lovely War!* and in the 2006 film *Merry Christmas*. (See **Wartime Christmases**)

Church of the Holy Nativity The church in Bethlehem which derives its name from the fact that it is believed to be built over the exact place where Jesus* was born. The traditional birthplace, a small cavern which had served as a stable, probably underneath a house (see **Bethlehem**), was visited by Saint Helena, the mother of Constantine, the first Christian Emperor of Rome. In 330 AD he built the first church over the cavern, and in order to do so had to pull down a temple to Adonis built there by the anti-Christian Emperor Hadrian (117-138 AD) in order to defile what must already have been a Christian shrine.

Soon after the building of the first church here – the oldest known church in the world – the great scholar St Jerome spent 30 years working in the cavern on his translation of the Hebrew and Greek scriptures into the Latin version known as the Vulgate. For most of its history the Church of the Holy Nativity has been a most important place of pilgrimage, honoured by royalty. Edward III, for example, is said to have provided roof timbers from his royal Forest of Knaresborough in Yorkshire.

The very low, small entrance (designed to keep out soldiers on horseback), known as the Door of Humility, leads to a spacious church, in which steps lead down to the traditional birthplace of Jesus – a simple grotto about 3.5 x 13 metres. Over the centuries a series of ornate buildings have been built above and around it, and the Church of the Holy Nativity is now administered jointly by the Roman Catholic, Greek Orthodox and Armenian Churches. On the floor of the cavern is a silver star around which is a Latin inscription informing pilgrims and visitors that 'Here Jesus Christ was born of the Virgin Mary*'. This is said to mark the exact place where the birth occurred, and its temporary removal sparked off a quarrel between France* and Russia* which, ironically, helped to start the Crimean War of 1854. (See **Nativity**)

Cock-crow The old folklore that the cock crows throughout the night on Christmas Eve is referred to by Shakespeare in the opening scene of *Hamlet* '… the bird of dawning singeth all night long'. (See also **Plygain**)

Cole, Henry (1808-82) The man who had the idea of producing the first commercial Christmas card, a thousand of which were printed for him in 1843, designed by J.C. Horsley. Henry Cole, of South Kensington, later Sir Henry Cole, was a friend of Queen Victoria* and Prince Albert* and a prominent figure in the Society of Arts. He organized the Great Exhibition of 1851, founded the Victoria and Albert Museum in 1852, and opened Britain's first public toilets. For his many services to civilized living he was knighted in 1875. (See **Christmas Cards, Horsley, J.C.**)

Coventry Carol Originally a sorrowful lullaby sung by the women of Bethlehem* in the Coventry cycle mystery play*, *The Pageant of Shearers and Tailors*, performed before Queen Margaret at Coventry in 1546. It is a lament for the children slaughtered on the orders of Herod*:

> Herod the king,
> In his raging,
> Chargèd he hath this day

His men of might,
In his own sight
All young children to slay.

(See **Holy Innocents**)

Cradle-rocking (See **Candlemas**)

Cradled in a manger meanly Written by the Methodist minister George S. Rowe (1830-1913), this hymn includes the line 'Who have winter, but no Christmas', anticipating the phrase used by C.S. Lewis in *The Chronicles of Narnia*.

Cranberries These sharp-flavoured red berries, rich in Vitamin C, were said to have been found growing in the area where the Pilgrim Fathers also found turkeys*. As cranberry sauce they have become a standard accompaniment to roast turkey.

Crib Strictly speaking, this word refers to the cot or cradle in which the Christ-child was laid, the manger* referred to by St Luke. In popular use it refers to the nativity scene, a group of model figures which include Mary*, Joseph*, and the baby in the manger. (See **Nativity Scene, Santons**)

Crib Friends An international association, founded in 1953 to promote interest in the setting up of a crib or nativity scene in homes and churches.

Crowns, paper The typical paper hats found in crackers and worn at Christmas parties seem to have originated in the paper crowns worn as a reminder of the Three Kings. (See **France**)

Dancing An expression of joy through dancing has long been associated with Christmas, ranging from folk-dancing, boys dancing in Seville Cathedral and priests celebrating in Ethiopia, to formal dancing at court and in traditional Christmas ballets such as *The Nutcracker**. A curious old West Country carol, 'Tomorrow shall be my dancing day', even depicts Jesus* celebrating his birth as a kind of Lord of the Dance, and 'The Twelve Days of Christmas' has 'nine ladies dancing'. (See **Sword Dancing**)

Decorations Ever since human beings first made an attempt to brighten up the gloom of the winter solstice*, homes have been decorated with whatever green and colourful plants were available. (See **Evergreens**) The present widespread use of such Christmas decorations as holly*, ivy*, mistletoe*, fir cones and the Christmas tree is amongst the most ancient of traditions. Coloured cloth or paper was used to brighten up the early nativity scenes*, especially in Italy*, and the yule-log* used to be decorated with gaily coloured ribbons. But paper-chains (originally home-made), streamers, paper bells,

bauble* ornaments for Christmas trees, balloons etc. have been increasingly used. Since the end of the nineteenth century electric fairy lights have become standard, and multicoloured illuminations are now common, both indoors and out.

Christmas decorations are traditionally removed once Epiphany* is over, though in earlier times they were left until Candlemas*. (See also **Advent Calendar, Angel Chimes, Candles, Christmas Cactus, Christmas Tree, Christmas Cards, Kissing Bough, Nativity Light** etc.)

Devil's Knell Tolling the Devil's Knell is a remarkable custom which takes place in the Parish Church of All Saints, Dewsbury in West Yorkshire, every Christmas Eve. The tradition is that when Jesus* was born the Devil in effect died, so his death-knell is tolled on the tenor bell of the church. What the locals sometimes call 't'Owd Lad's Passin' Bell' is tolled once for every year since the birth of Christ*. The inaccuracy in the calendar (see **Christmas Day**) is ignored and the bell is pulled according to the number of the year, e.g. 2006 times. The whole sequence is timed to end on the stroke of midnight. Each stroke is noted and signed by a ringer. Another explanation of the custom is that it started in the Middle Ages as an attempt to drive Satan away from Dewsbury for another year. According to legend the bell was given by a local nobleman, Sir Thomas de Soothill, at the end of the thirteenth century. He is said to have presented it as a penance for having murdered one of his servants and having thrown the body into a dam, and the tenor bell carries a reminder of this in its name, 'Black Tom'. The Royal Mail issued a stamp depicting the Devil's Knell for Christmas 1986.

Dia de Reyes (See **Epiphany**)

Dickens, Charles (1812-70) The great Victorian novelist was so enthusiastic about the keeping of Christmas and so persuasive an advocate in his writing – both in the UK and in America – that it has even been said that Dickens 'invented' our modern Christmas. Along with Queen Victoria* and Prince Albert*, he certainly gave the revival of Christmas a tremendous boost, especially by his portrayal of merry family gatherings enjoying their Christmas fare and entertainment with enormous gusto. In his *Sketches by Boz*, several of his novels and short stories, he delights in creating an old-word Christmas atmosphere, from the party at Dingley Dell in *Pickwick Papers* to the Christmas dinner presided over by Uncle Pumblechook in *Great Expectations*.

Dickens also encouraged the telling of ghost stories at Christmas-time. In addition to several short stories, his best-known Christmas goblins and spirits appear in *Pickwick Papers* (1837) and in *A Christmas Carol* (1843). The latter was the most influential of his Christmas writings, and did much to establish the festival as a time of concern for the underprivileged, when it is unthinkable to behave like the mean-spirited Scrooge. Following its success Dickens aimed at producing a Christmas story each year, and in 1852 published a collection of five as *Christmas Books*, with a festive tale every year in his magazine, *Household Words* (from 1856), and his posthumous collection *Christmas Stories* (1874). There is a Dickens Festival each Christmas at Malton, North Yorkshire, where Dickens stayed, and the annual re-enactment at Rochester, Kent, of his 'Six Poor Travellers' (1854). (See **A Christmas Carol, Christmas Tree, Ghosts, Pickwick Papers, Scrooge, Tiny Tim**)

Drinks Alcoholic drinks seem such an important source of Christmas conviviality to many people that it has been rightly said that their Christmas

50

spirit 'comes out of bottles'. Attitudes to alcohol range from total abstinence, through temperate and moderate festive drinking, to the excessive consumption of binge-drinkers and the drink-related crimes and accidents which can turn Christmas celebrations into horrific tragedies. For abstainers there are many alternatives, such as non-alcoholic kinds of ginger wine. (For drinks traditionally associated with Christmas see **Ale Posset, Bishop, Brandy, Egg-Nog, Mead, Mulled Wine, Port, Punch, Rum, Sherry, Wassail Bowl**)

Druids These priests, healers and general leaders of the Celtic people of Ancient Britain are associated with Christmas through their ceremony at the winter solstice*, when they cut the sacred mistletoe. The present Most Ancient Order of Druids is a revival movement founded in 1717. (See **Mistletoe**)

Dumb Cake A cake traditionally baked on Christmas Eve by an unmarried girl in search of her true love. She was supposed to make it in absolute silence – hence the name – and fast from all food throughout Christmas Eve. She would then prick her initials into the top of the Dumb Cake and leave it in the hearth to bake. The door was left open in the hope that at midnight an apparition of her future husband would enter and either turn the cake or leave his initials on top.

Egg Nog A traditional Christmas drink consisting of hot, spiced ale (or cider in Devon, where it is called Egg Hot), to which have been added eggs, milk or cream and sugar. Its popularity in America is shown by the Egg Nog Riot in 1826, when the superintendent of West Point banned all alcoholic drinks at Christmas, and 19 army cadets were court-martialled for rioting. In the southern states Egg Nog is known as Southern Comfort.

Egypt Because Mary* and Joseph* fled from the wrath of Herod*, travelling from Bethlehem* to the safety of Egypt (Matthew 2.13-15), there has been a strong Christian tradition in this otherwise Muslim country, still represented by the surviving Coptic Church. Coptic Christians prepare to celebrate Christmas by fasting from meat and using Advent* as a time of solemn prayer and charity*. The Church of Abu Sergah in Old Cairo is said to be built over a cave where the Holy Family rested, and six miles away at Mataria a garden is the traditional site of where they stayed.

El Niño Meaning 'the Christ-child' in Spanish, this term is used to describe a warm current in the Pacific Ocean, which often appears near the coast of Peru and Ecuador during the Christmas season, causing disturbances in the weather.

Emmanuel (See **Immanuel**)

Epiphany The Church festival held on 6 January, which commemorates the visit of the Wise Men*, and is known in Ireland as 'Little Christmas'. It was originally used by the Eastern Church to celebrate the nativity* and baptism of Jesus*, and its name, derived from the Greek *epiphaneia* (manifestation), refers to the showing of Jesus to the Gentiles, i.e. non-Jews, in the person of the Magi*. Epiphany is the Twelfth Day of Christmas, and the occasion of church services and parties to round off the Christmas season, especially in France* and Spain*. (See **Dia de Reyes, Fête des Rois, Frankincense, Haxey Hood Game, Magi, Myrrh, Old Christmas Day, Twelfth Night, Wise Men**)

Es ist ein' Ros' entsprungen A beautiful German carol* dating from the fifteenth century, a common translation beginning: 'The Noble Stem of Jesse hath flowered on this tide'. (See **Jesse Tree**)

Ethiopia Members of the ancient Coptic Church of Ethiopia prepare for Christmas by keeping a fast for 43 days. Christmas Day* (7 January) is a time of feasting, dancing* and the giving of presents to children*. There is also a kind of hockey, supposed to originate from a game played by the shepherds* when Jesus* was born.

Evergreens A great variety of evergreen shrubs and trees were used as decorations during the Roman* midwinter festivals of Saturnalia*, Kalends* and Yule-tide*, and their use continued during the festival of Christmas which replaced them. They brightened up the gloomy winter with their glossy green leaves and bright berries, but were also a symbol of continuing life, when most of nature appeared dead. Many kinds of evergreens were originally used: bay*, rosemary*, box, yew, holly*, ivy*, mistletoe*, and various coniferous trees such as cypress and fir, the latter eventually taking over as the principal decoration. (See **Christmas Tree**) Even as late as the end of the sixteenth century there was greater variety of evergreens than is seen at Christmas today. John Stow (1598) records that 'Against the time of Christmas every man's house, as also their parish churches, were decked with holme (holly), ivie, bayes, and whatsoever the season afforded to be greene'. Evergreens and, indeed, all forms of decoration* are traditionally removed after Twelfth Night* to avert bad luck, though an earlier tradition allowed them to remain in the house until Candlemas*. (See **Christmas, Gregory the Great, Wreaths**)

Plate 1:
The Adoration of the Shepherds by Guido Reni (1575-1642),
The National Gallery, London

Plate 2:
The Adoration of the Magi by Peter Paul Rubens (1577-1640),
King's College Cambridge

CHRISTMAS TREE AT WINDSOR CASTLE.—DRAWN BY J. L. WILLIAMS.—(SEE NEXT PAGE.)

Plate 3:
Christmas tree at Windsor Castle – drawn by J. L. Williams
from *The Illustrated London News*, 1848

Plate 4:
Top – Entrance to the Church of the Holy Nativity, Bethlehem.
These Arab Christian children need not bend low at the Door of Humility.

Bottom – The Silver Star, Church of the Holy Nativity,
said to mark the place where Jesus was born.

Plate 5:
Top – The Author's Family Nativity Scene. Hand-painted figures set up in 1956

Bottom – Santa Claus visited by Molly, the author's granddaughter
(then aged two and a half)

Plate 6:
Top – The First Christmas Card (1843).
This copy is signed by the artist, J. C. Horsley.

Bottom – The First Christmas Cracker, as depicted
in *The Illustrated London News*, 1847

Plate 7:
Top Left – Martin Luther
Top Right – Charles Wesley
Bottom Left – Charles Dickens
Bottom Right – Queen Victoria

BASSANO
PHOTO.
VICTORIA QUEEN OF GREAT BRITAIN
G. R. & CO.
LONDON.
EMPRESS OF INDIA
1837—JUBILEE—1887.

Plate 8:
Queen Elizabeth II making her first Christmas Day Broadcast to her people in the
United Kingdom and throughout the world at Sandringham House, Norfolk.
Picture by PA/EMPICS

Father Christmas Although Father Christmas is now an alternative name for Santa Claus, originally St Nicholas*, there is no doubt that for many centuries he was a figure who existed independently of St Nicholas, and that the complete blending of the two traditions did not take place until the second half of the nineteenth century. Even today some countries distinguish between the two by keeping up the tradition of the visit of St Nicholas on 6 December, St Nicholas's Day, or on the 5 December, St Nicholas' Eve. (See **Holland, Germany**)

Although the Santa Claus tradition dates back to the fourth century, when St Nicholas lived, the origin of Father Christmas may well go back to prehistoric times, to some ancient Nordic god such as Odin*, the bearded bringer of gifts, who was worshipped especially during the festival of the winter solstice*. References to Christmas personified occur as early as the fifteenth century, and he was an important character in the traditional plays performed by mummers*, several of which open with the lines:

> Here comes I, old Father Christmas,
> Be I welcome, or welcome not;
> I hope old Father Christmas
> Will never be forgot.

The character was familiar enough to open the play, *Christmas his Masque* (1616), written by Ben Jonson for the Christmas of James I. Later in the seventeenth century an attempt was made in both England and America to abolish Father Christmas, as part of the general condemnation of Christians as a pagan and popish ritual. (See **Puritans**) He survived, however, and a cartoon in the pamphlet, *The Vindication of Christmas* (1653), shows the robed and bearded figure of Old Christmas

Imprinted at London for G. Horton 1653.2

appealing to a Puritan, who had told him to go away: 'O Sir, I bring good cheere!' In early Victorian England, before the arrival of the Santa Claus tradition from America, the notion of Father Christmas was encouraged by Charles Dickens*, whose tremendously influential story, *A Christmas Carol*, describes him in the guise of 'the Spirit of Christmas Past, Present and Future'.

In modern times further attempts have been made to abolish Father Christmas. Communist countries, embarrassed by the Christian origin of

Santa Claus (ironically, St Nicholas is the patron saint of Russia*) replaced him with 'Grandfather Frost'. On the other hand, Catholic countries, upset by the non-Christian elements dominating Christmas, have also tried to abolish him; an effigy of Father Christmas was publicly hanged and burnt in front of Dijon Cathedral as recently as 1951.

There is no doubt, however, that Father Christmas is alive and well, now firmly established all over the world, whether in the heat of an Australian* December, where he arrives by boat on Sydney's Bondi Beach, or in the cold of a northern winter, where he is enthroned in department stores everywhere. Even his fictitious home can be visited – parents take their children* by plane to Lapland, in an expensive commercial exploitation of the fairy tale. And, as the most powerful surviving figure of folklore, Father Christmas, alias Santa Claus, is likely to thrill young children till the end of time. (See **Christmas Stocking, Saint Nicholas, Santa Claus**)

Father Christmas Cartoon story by Raymond Briggs, published in 1973. (See **Snowman**)

Feast of Fools (See **Lord of Misrule**)

Feast of Stephen A phrase familiar through J.M. Neale's carol* about Good King Wenceslas*, who performed his work of charity* and hospitality 'on the feast of Stephen'. This is, in fact, the same day as Boxing Day*, and the 26 December has been kept at St Stephen's Day since as early as the fourth century, when Stephen was accorded the great honour of having his commemoration the day after the birthday of Jesus*. St Stephen was the first Christian martyr, who died asking that his murderers might be forgiven (Acts 7.60). His faith had a great influence on Saul of Tarsus (later the Apostle Paul) who was present when he died. For some curious reason St Stephen's Day was always chosen as the day for another kind of martyrdom, the custom of 'Hunting the Wren'. (See **Wren**) Also difficult to explain is the connection of St Stephen with horses, and the old custom of ceremonially galloping, feeding, decorating and then bleeding horses on St Stephen's Day to ensure that they would thrive in the New Year.

In Sweden it was once the custom for horse riders known as 'Stephen's men' to race each other and rouse the villages with singing and shouting on this day. Since the first St Stephen appears to have had no connection with horses it may be that there has been a confusion with an eleventh-century Stephen who preached the gospel in Sweden and was martyred there. However, there could still be a reminder of the bloody death of the first Christian martyr in the blood-letting of horses, and hunting in general. Last century, for example, in Wales and Scotland there was the St Stephen's Day custom of Holming Day*, when boys used to beat each other with holly* until the blood ran.

Festival of Nine Lessons and Carols A service which traces the story of the coming of the Christ* in nine Scripture readings, starting with the first hint of the gospel in the 'protevangelium' (Genesis 3.8-15), going through various prophecies to the story of the nativity* in the Gospels of St Luke and St Matthew, and ending with the majestic prologue of St John's Gospel. Interspersed with these are nine carols*, traditionally sung by candlelight. The first verse of the first carol, 'Once in royal David's city'*, is sung by a boy soprano (who at King's College is chosen just before the service begins) and the last carol is 'Hark! The herald angels sing'*.

The Festival of Nine Lessons and Carols was first drawn up in 1878 by Bishop E.H. Benson (later Archbishop of Canterbury), when he was Bishop of Truro, for use in Truro Cathedral. It was later borrowed and simplified by the Very Reverend E. Milner-White, Dean of King's College, Cambridge, who also wrote the Bidding Prayer. Although now performed in many cathedrals and churches, it is inextricably linked with the chapel of King's College*, Cambridge, where it was first performed in 1918, and from where its superlative singing has been broadcast every Christmas Eve since 1928.

Fête des Rois (See **France**)

Figgy Pudding (See **Fruit**)

Films Films are now an established part of Christmas for many people, both in the cinema and on television, particularly in the afternoon of Christmas Day*. These include classics such as *The Wizard of Oz* (1939), and various Disney, James Bond and Spielberg films, for example. Box office successes which have a specific reference to Christmas include the following: *Holiday Inn* (1942) (see **White Christmas**), *It's a Wonderful Life* (1946), *Miracle on 34th Street* (1947), *A Christmas Carol* (1951) (with Alastair Sim as Scrooge*), *White Christmas* (1954), *Santa Claus: the Movie* (1985), *Home Alone* (1990), *The Santa Clause* (1994), *Merry Christmas* (2006).

Finland Finland has its own well-established traditions, such as the gift-bringer *Joulupukki**, the annual custom of declaring the 'Christmas Peace' at the old capital of Turku, and the popular parties known as *pikkijoulu* (Little Christmas). But Finland has also successfully cashed in on the modern fashion to encourage children* to write to, and even visit, the real Santa Claus at his home near the Arctic Circle in Finnish Lapland, where snow and reindeer are guaranteed. (See **Santa Claus**)

First Footing The custom of making sure that the first person to enter the house in the New Year is one who will bring good luck. In Britain, especially in the north and in Scotland, the First Footer is traditionally a dark-haired, handsome, unmarried young man, bringing a piece of coal, and sometimes bread, salt, money etc., as symbols of prosperity for the coming year. Customs vary according to the region. In the Flamborough district on the North Yorkshire coast, for example, the First Foot used to be given wine, money and Peppercake*. (See **Hogmanay, New Year**)

First Nowell Using the word for Christmas still used by the French (see **Nowell**), this is an anonymous English carol* of very early date, collected by William Sandys in 1833. In very simple language it tells the story of the nativity* and its meaning.

Flap-Dragon A traditional Christmas game which is a kind of West Country variant of snapdragon*. The players each attempt to drink from a can of cider in the centre of which is a burning candle*.

Flight into Egypt The term used for the hurried escape from the wrath of Herod* by Mary* and Joseph*, with their baby (Matthew 2.13-15). Their 'flight' was quite misunderstood by the little Sunday school boy who drew a picture of four figures in an aeroplane. On being asked who the fourth figure was he is supposed to have replied: 'That's Pontius, the pilot.' (See **Egypt**)

Flowers In addition to evergreens*, flowers often form part of Christmas decorations*, not only those in bloom at this time, such as winter jasmine, chrysanthemums, Christmas Roses or the Christmas Cactus, but others specially grown. In earlier times, especially in the eighteenth century, it was usual to have artificial flowers at Christmas, including some delicately made of tinted sugar. (See **Christmas Cherry, Christmas Rose, Poinsettia, Zygocactus**)

Food From the earliest prehistoric midwinter festivals to the modern Christmas special kinds of food – often sumptuous dishes and usually in abundance – have been central to the celebrations. There has, however, been a gradual change in the type of food. Probably the oldest traditional meat is roast pork*, which dates back to Roman* and Scandinavian* times, and which is maintained in the boar's head* feasts and in the custom of having at Christmas a joint of pork*, as well as ham, brawn, stand pies, chipolata sausages (with turkey) etc. Other well-established meats were roast beef, a standard item on the Christmas table in the eighteenth and nineteenth centuries, and roast venison*. 'Humble pie', for the poor, was made from umbles, the offal of venison. Originally all Christmas pies appear to have been savoury, filled with minced meat, game and poultry. Spices and fruit were added, and eventually these predominated, as in the modern mince pie*. Even plum pudding started life as a first-course savoury dish. (See **Christmas Pie, Christmas Pudding**)

Poultry has always been important at Christmas, and seems to have reached its peak, both in variety and quantity, in Tudor times, when we read of banquets including, geese, ducks, pheasants, partridges, capons (fattened cockerels), bustards, herons, cranes, swans, guinea fowl and peacocks – which were served with full plumage and gilded beaks – and finally turkeys. Lavish dinners were enjoyed by royalty and by the wealthy. In 1500, for example, Henry VII ordered a Christmas dinner with 120 different dishes. In 1512 Henry VIII 'kept his Christmasse at Greenwich, when there was such an abundance of viands served to all comers of any honest behaviour'.

As a reaction to the banning of feasts by the Puritans* there was eventually a return to gargantuan meals, such as one in Bristol at Christmas 1788, which included fish (cod, turbot, brill, soles, plaice, herrings, eels, carp, perch, salmon), game (hare, pheasant, grouse, partridge, wild ducks and geese, moorhens, curlews, bitterns, woodcock, snipe, plovers, pigeons), poultry (chickens, capons, ducks, geese, turkeys), roast meat (beef, veal, pork, mutton), and odds and ends such as oysters, steaks, chops, sausages, brawn, ham, tongue, pies, tarts and jellies.

For ordinary folk the main dish was likely to be a chicken, or for a larger family, a goose*, the Christmas dish of the Crachit family in Charles Dickens's *A Christmas Carol*, though they were also sent a turkey by the reformed Scrooge*. Whether turkey, goose, pork or beef, the Christmas meat in earlier days, especially in Victorian times, was likely to be cooked in a communal oven at the baker's, as few families had ovens big enough at home. The tremendous amount of food roasted and baked at this time led the Italians to say of somebody exceptionally busy: *Ha più da fare che i forni di Natale in Inghilterra* (He's more to do than English ovens at Christmas).

The Victorians – or at least those in the middle classes – appear to have had as much variety of Christmas food as the Tudors. In *A Christmas Carol* there are sucking-pigs, sausages, barrels of oysters*, roast chestnuts*, apples*, oranges*, lemons, pears, grapes, filberts (hazel nuts), onions, almonds, raisins, sticks of cinnamon, candied fruits, figs, French plums, tea and coffee, in addition to meat, game and poultry.

Several of the traditional Christmas dishes, such as frumenty*, have now almost entirely disappeared, but the average family usually enjoys the basic minimum of roast turkey and Christmas pudding, as well as some form of pork, and a variety of desserts, including mince pies*, Christmas cake*, trifle* and fruits and sweetmeats such as dates, figs, nuts, ginger, Turkish delight*, chocolate etc.. (See also **Drinks**, **Fruits**, **Goose**, **Marrons Glacés**, **Peppercake**, **Spices**, **Turkey** etc.)

Fourth Wise Man The legendary wise man who spent so much time on his journey caring for the sick and the poor that he arrived in the Holy Land only in time to see Jesus crucified. This was the basis of the story, *The Other Wise Man* (1896), first read as a sermon by the New York Presbyterian minister, the Revd Henry Van Dyke.

France   In France, as in other Catholic countries, the nativity scene* or crib*, *la crèche* – with its little carved wooden figures known as *santons** – has a more central place in homes and churches than the Christmas tree, introduced into Paris in about 1840 from Protestant Germany, and popular as *le sapin de Noël*.

On Christmas Eve, *la Veille de Noël*, it is an old custom for French children* to place their shoes, originally wooden *sabots*, in front of the fireplace, or in some other convenient place, where they will be filled with presents during the night. Some families have the tradition that the gifts are brought by St Nicholas* or Father Christmas*, *le Père Noël*, others that they are brought by the Christ-child, *l'Enfant Jésus*. An old tradition is that the gift-bringer is accompanied by *le Père Fouettard**, who punishes children who have been naughty.

In France attendance at *la Messe de Minuit* on Christmas Eve is often followed by a special meal known as *le Réveillon**, though this may be deferred till a later hour on Christmas Day. Traditional French food for Christmas is goose*, though this is now usually replaced by turkey*, and the French insist on a female one, *la dinde*, not *le dindon*, as they consider it more tender! Other traditional dishes are oysters* at the *Réveillon*, truffles and *pâté de foie gras*, a rich paste made from goose or duck liver. Popular sweets are *la bûche de Noel**, a kind of chocolate log, and *marrons glacés**. A typical Christmas cheese is *Vacherin*.

New Year's Day, *le Jour de l' An,* is the traditional time for the exchange of greetings-cards and presents, the latter known as *étrennes* (derived from the Latin word for the presents or *strenae* exchanged during Saturnalia* and Kalends*). Epiphany*, 6 January, is kept as *la Fête des Rois*, in honour of the Three Kings. Their visit is commemorated by a meal which includes *une galette,* a kind of flat cake containing a bean or tiny doll representing the Christ-child. Whoever finds this in his or her portion becomes king or queen, wearing a paper crown, choosing a royal partner, and presiding over the festivities. (See also **Carols**)

Francis of Assisi (See **St Francis**)

Frankincense The second of the three gifts presented by the Wise Men to the Christ-child (Matthew 2.11). The word comes from Old French *franc encens*, i.e. true, or best quality, incense. It is obtained from various aromatic shrubs and resinous trees of the Boswellia genus (named after Johnson's biographer), reduced to yellowish crystals, and has been associated with religious worship from remotest times, so that the prophet Jeremiah (seventh century BC) is able to refer to 'incense from Sheba' (Jeremiah 6.20). The use of incense in Christian worship is not mentioned until about 500 AD, but the presentation of frankincense to the baby Jesus* has always been regarded as a symbolic recognition of his deity – the smoke rising as in prayer to God. Along with gold* and myrrh*, frankincense is presented on behalf of the Queen* during the Epiphany* ceremony in the Chapel Royal, St James's Palace, London. (See **Wise Men**)

Fruit Fruit has always been an essential part of Christmas fare, especially the more exotic kinds which remind us of the eastern origins of Christmas. Apples* have a long association with pork* and wassailing*. An orange* is sometimes used instead of an apple in the mouth of the boar's head*, and also accompanies the apple (and a new penny) in the traditional Christmas stocking. Of the various dried fruits raisins – sometimes referred to as 'plums' in old recipes – are perhaps most closely associated with Christmas, being used in Christmas puddings and cakes, and also in the game of snapdragon*.

Of the fruits which come from the land where Jesus* was born, pomegranates, dates (traditionally in characteristic oval boxes) and figs have for centuries made a contribution to Christmas. Figs were once a popular ingredient of boiled puddings, as is shown by the Old West Country song, 'We wish you a Merry Christmas', with its demand:

> We all like figgy pudding,
> So bring some out here!

As well as raisins, other varieties of dried grapes are currants from Greece and sultanas from Turkey. Along with candied peel they are used in enormous quantities in the mince pies, puddings and cakes of the festive season.

Frumenty Derived from the Old French *frument* (wheat), frumenty, frumity or furmenty is an old Christmas dish, still prepared in some country districts, based on wheat that has been crushed, hulled (i.e. the husks removed) and then simmered with milk, egg yolks etc. and flavoured with sugar and spices* such as nutmeg, cinnamon or cloves, and with the addition of currants. Frumenty was usually eaten on its own, served piping hot in special bowls on Christmas Eve. It was also served with mutton and especially venison*.

Gabriel The angel* so named in St Luke's Gospel, who appeared to Mary* with the message that she was to be the mother of the Messiah*. The name in Hebrew means 'man of God'. Gabriel is mentioned in the Old Testament twice, appearing to Daniel (Daniel 8.15 and 9.21). In the New Testament he also appears to Zacharias, the father of John the Baptist (Luke 1.19). The 'angel of the Lord' who appears to Joseph* and later to the shepherds* is usually taken to be Gabriel. His festival day is 24 March, the day before Lady Day, which commemorates his visit to Mary. The Angel Gabriel is mentioned in several carols*, and is the subject of a beautiful Basque* carol. (See **Annunciation**)

Games In past days various games had a traditional association with Christmas. By the end of the seventeenth century these included billiards, bowls, tennis, and various gambling games, especially with cards and dice. From accounts of Christmas parties in the eighteenth century we know that in addition to a variety of dances, it was the custom, for example, to play blind man's buff, a game already very old, and still going strong in the following century, as we learn from Charles Dickens* in his description of the Christmas Eve party at Dingley Dell. (See **Pickwick Papers**) Other lively games included ducking for apples* in a tub of water, jumping up to try to reach cakes dipped in treacle, snapdragon* and mimes such as Dumb Crambo. In more recent years there have been all kinds of party games: musical chairs, charades, postman's knock, sardines, murder, balloon games etc.

Card games date back to at least the reign of Edward IV, when a law was passed which restricted card-playing to the Christmas holiday. By the beginning of the nineteenth century special cards were being devised, rather like Happy Families, with characters such as Mr Lovemoney, Captain Kill-All and Miss Bookworm (1823), and educational games with countries, and cards with riddles, such as the board game of Toby Tott and his Christmas Pudding (1845) and the Indian board game of Pachisi (1867).

In the present century, in addition to the standard favourites of chess and draughts, the mass production of board games has found its most important market at Christmas, though attractively produced boxed games are gradually being displaced by play stations and other sophisticated electronic entertainments. (For a chronological list see **Toys and Games**)

Germany Along with Advent calendars* and wreaths* the German build-up to Christmas is seen in the famous Christmas markets, the oldest of which were held in Dresden (1434) and Nuremberg (1559), the latter traditionally opened by a girl representing the *Christkind* (Christ-child). In the more Catholic southern parts of Germany and in Austria* there are processions known as the *Frauentragen* and the *Herbergsuchen,* re-enacting the Holy Family's search for a safe lodging. In these parts the nativity scene* or crib*, *die Krippe,* predominates. In the more Protestant northern parts the Christmas tree*, *der Tannenbaum,* is central to the festivities. On the 6 December the children* are visited by *Sankt Klaus* (St Nicholas*), who has a sack of presents in his right hand, and in his left is supposed to hold a birch rod to beat children who have been naughty. To help him he traditionally has a fierce-looking assistant dressed in skins or straw, known as *Knecht Ruprecht*, Krampus*,* or other names according to the region. It is still customary to decorate the tree with actual candles*, which are lit on *Heiliger Abend*, Christmas Eve, when the Germans gather round the tree to give out the presents, and the children receive gifts from *der Weihnachtsmann,* Father Christmas*, or in Catholic families *das Christkind*.

Outside Germany the best-known food specialities for Christmas are *Lebkuchen* and *Stollen.* New Year's Eve, *der Silvesterabend,* is also a time for festivity, as is Twelfth Night*, when some families commemorate the visit of the three kings by eating a *Dreikönigskuchen,* a cake in which a thimble is hidden. As in the French custom, whoever finds this becomes king or queen, presiding over the festival. (See **Advent Calendar, Advent Wreath, Albert, Carols, Luther, O Tannenbaum, Es ist ein' Ros' entsprungen**)

Ghosts Paradoxically, Christmas – the joyful season of peace and good will – is also the traditional season for the telling of ghost stories. The origin of this can be traced to the prehistoric ceremonies connected with the winter solstice*, when the long, dark nights held supernatural terrors for primitive humankind. In modern days ghost stories can be enjoyed in the warmth of home, with the experience heightened by the contrast of the cold and dark outside.

Charles Dickens* did much to encourage the custom of telling such tales at Christmas-time. His *Pickwick Papers** (1837) contains an account of one such story, 'The Goblins who Stole a Sexton', told on Christmas Eve, and later he wrote a series of ghost stories. His most famous contribution, of course, is in *A Christmas Carol** (1843), subtitled 'A Ghost Story for Christmas', in which Scrooge* is visited by the three famous spectres of Christmas Past, Present and Future.

The Gifts of the Magi The famous short story by the American author, O'Henry, written for Christmas 1906, its surprise ending influenced by the stories of Maupassant.

Glastonbury Thorn The Holy Thorn of Glastonbury Abbey, Somerset, is famous because it flowers around Christmas Day*, and every year sprays from the tree are sent to be placed on the Queen's* table at Christmas. Glastonbury Abbey is probably the oldest in the British Isles, and ancient legend (not actually written down until the early twelfth century) ascribes its foundation to Joseph of Arimathea, the rich councillor who obtained permission from Pilate to bury Jesus* in his family tomb (Mark 15:43). When Joseph supposedly reached Glastonbury, bringing with him the Holy Grail, it is said that on Christmas Eve he stuck his staff in the ground, where it took root and grew, and has miraculously flowered every year since at Christmas time in honour of the birth of Jesus.

The Glastonbury Thorn is a species of hawthorn (*Crataegus monogyna praecox*) which flowers in May and also in December, or very early January. The original tree was chopped down by Puritans* on the orders of Oliver Cromwell, who regarded the veneration of the Holy Thorn as idolatrous. The man who actually chopped it down is said to have been blinded when a chip of wood struck him in the eye. Cuttings were taken from the ancient tree, and a substantial Glastonbury Thorn survived until 1991, now continued in further cuttings. A similar thorn, probably a cutting from Glastonbury, blooms around Christmas at Orcrop in Herefordshire.

In the late eighteenth century, especially, great crowds assembled at Glastonbury to see the Christmas blossoms. After the change in the calendar in 1752 they usually found that it still continued to bloom on Old Christmas Day (6 January).

Gloria in excelsis (See **Angel**)

Go tell it on the mountain An American carol* that is a kind of Negro spiritual, collected by the black musician F.J. Work (1880-1942).

God rest you merry, gentlemen One of the best traditional English carols*, of unknown origin. Old when mentioned by Charles Dickens* in *A Christmas Carol*, it may date back to the sixteenth century.

Gold The most familiar of the gifts presented by the Wise Men*, understood as a symbol of royalty, a tribute to the child 'born King of the Jews' (Matthew 2.2). Since at least 2,500 BC gold has been prized for its beauty and untarnished durability. Its most common use was as coins, money that could have helped the refugee family during the flight into Egypt*.

Good Christian men, rejoice (See **In Dulci Jubilo**)

Good Will Although the term is commonly used at Christmas (e.g. 'the season of good will') few realize that the angelic message of 'good will towards people on whom his favour rests' (Luke 2.14) refers to the benevolence of

God towards humanity, revealed in the coming of Christ*. However, as a necessary response to this, Christians also use the term to mean a special effort to be kind and caring at Christmas.

Goose The standard Christmas poultry before turkey* took over, its popularity said to have been increased at Christmas 1588, when Queen Elizabeth I, dining on goose, was given details of the Spanish Armada. The place of goose as an essential Christmas dish is shown by the old rhyme beginning:

> Christmas is coming, the geese are getting fat,
> Please to put a penny in the old man's hat.

Flocks of geese were often driven many miles to market, and their feet were actually shod for the journey, as with Norfolk turkeys. In Victorian times poor families would save up for Christmas by paying into a 'goose club'. The bird was still an important dish in 1892, when a Christmas goose featured in the Sherlock Holmes story 'The Blue Carbuncle'. (See **A Christmas Carol**)

Gregory the Great Pope Gregory I (540-604 AD) could be said to have contributed to the evolution of Christmas by encouraging people to adapt rather than destroy pagan customs, investing them with a Christian meaning. He also sent Augustine as a missionary to England, where Christmas was used for the great mass baptism of 597 AD. (See **Christmas Day**)

Grinch A kind of American modern-day Scrooge*, this fairy-tale character originated in the story by Dr Seuss, *How the Grinch Stole Christmas* (1957).

Groundhog Day (See **Candlemas**)

Guisers Derived from the word 'disguise' this term is still used in parts of Britain for those who 'let in the New Year', especially in ancient traditions in Scotland, Northumberland and Cornwall. Guisers have blackened or covered faces and wear colourful costumes. (See **First Foot, Hogmanay, New Year, Up-Helly-Aa**)

Handbells The ringing of handbells at Christmas is an old custom sometimes associated with the parish church, sometimes with the Waits* or watchmen, who were also known as bellmen, because they rang a handbell as they called out the hour. The Waits were the first to usher in Christmas at midnight, with their ringing and singing.

Handsel Monday In Scotland the first Monday after Old New Year's Day (12 January), a traditional holiday mainly for farm workers, who received 'handsel' or gifts of money from their employers. (See **Boxing Day**)

Handel's Messiah This great oratorio by George Frederick Handel was composed in 1741 in a fever of inspiration lasting 24 days, when Handel said: 'I did think I did see all Heaven before me, and the great God himself.' He conducted the first performance in Dublin in 1742, using only 36 musicians and 24 singers. The crowded hall received it with 'exquisite delight', and one of the later performances so moved George II that he stood up during the 'Hallelujah Chorus', a custom which has been observed by audiences ever since.

Although only the 21 pieces of the First Part refer to the birth of Jesus*, *Messiah* is regularly performed at Christmas, especially by churches and choirs in the north of England, notably by the Huddersfield Choral Society. Particular favourites at Christmas are 'For unto us a Child is born', the Pastoral Symphony (before the reference to the shepherds*), 'Glory to God', 'Rejoice greatly!' and 'He shall feed His flock' – all beautiful melodies which many know by heart, and which some still follow in their family's copy of the score.

Hark! The herald angels sing One of the most popular of carols*, the words are by Charles Wesley, the great hymnwriter of the Methodist Revival. Published in 1739 as 'A Hymn for Christmas Day', the first line used the old word for 'sky', and was originally written:

Hark how all the welkin rings!

This was changed to its present form in the collection published by George Whitefield in 1753. A more recent change has been in the line 'Born as man, with man to dwell', some versions reading with 'men to dwell', conflicting with the general use of 'man' (mankind) in this and another line. From 1856 it became especially popular as a carol when it was set by the organist William Cummings to a melody by Mendelssohn, originally composed as the second piece in his *Festgesang*, a work for men's voices and brass. This was written in 1840 for a festival celebrating Gutenberg and the invention of printing, and although Mendelssohn later made an arrangement for four parts and suggested new words, he wrote that he thought it would never be suitable for 'sacred words'. How wrong he proved to be!

75

Haxey Hood Game A game of great antiquity involving curious items of folklore, which takes place on Old Christmas Day* (6 January) at the village of Haxey, near Epworth in Lincolnshire. It is generally agreed that it is a survival of some prehistoric rite connected with the winter solstice*, possibly involving human sacrifice, but there is a local legend which explains its origin as follows. One day in the thirteenth century the wife of Sir John de Mowbray was riding from church over Haxey Hill when she lost her scarlet hood, blown away in a gale. Twelve labourers who worked in the boggy fenland – and who were therefore known as Boggans – chased after it, and eventually caught it. As a reward Lady Mowbray is said to have left thirteen half-acres of land to the parish, to provide a hood, the origin of the 'hoods' now played for each year in memory of the event.

The Hood Game has 12 official players, or Boggans. Traditionally they wear red-flannel coats, or some garment patched with red, and hats decorated with red flowers, the colour said to be derived from the scarlet hood. The players are organized by King Boggan or Lord of the Hood, who carries a staff made from thirteen willows bound with thirteen bands. Another important character is the Fool, whose face is smeared with soot and red ochre, and who begins the game in the early afternoon by mounting the base of an old cross near Haxey Church, where he invites everyone to join in the game with an old rhyme in dialect:

> Hoose agin hoose, toon agin toon,
> If thoo meets a man, knock 'im doon,
> But dooan't 'urt 'im

While he is saying this a fire of damp straw is lit round him and he is enveloped in smoke – a little ceremony, probably a survival of a purification rite, known as Smoking the Fool. After a preliminary game with several hoods made of tight rolls of canvas, which the crowd try to get past the Boggans to their own part of the parish, the Hood Game proper begins at 4 p.m. In this the hood, known as the Sway or Leather, a piece of rope about two feet long encased in stout leather, is competed for in a kind of mammoth rugby scrum. The object of the game is to pull or carry the Sway (throwing and kicking are not allowed) to one of three inns, the landlord of which keeps the hood until the following year.

Herod (73-4 BC) Herod the Great was the most famous member of the Herod family, the Idumaeans (or Edomites, the non-Jewish descendants of Esau), who helped to rule Palestine for the Romans*. Appointed king of Judaea in 40 BC, Herod was called 'the Great' because of his ambitious rebuilding of the Temple of Jerusalem, of Massada and the port of Caesarea. He is also remembered for acts of appalling ruthlessness and cruelty, which included the murder of his brother-in-law, his wife and their two sons. The

Jewish historian Josephus said of him: 'He was no king, but the most cruel tyrant who ever ascended a throne.' St Matthew's story of Herod's order to massacre the Holy Innocents* after the visit of the Wise Men*, is absolutely in keeping with what we know of him from secular history. (See **Nativity**)

Hodening The ancient Christmas custom of revellers carrying round a Hodening Horse. Similar to the surviving Welsh tradition (see **Mari Lwyd**), it consisted of a party going from house to house with a horse's skull attached to a pole, carried by someone hidden under a sheet or blanket. The jaws, worked by string, could be opened and snapped shut. The sudden appearance of a Hodening Horse so frightened a woman at Broadstairs in Kent in 1839 that she collapsed and died, causing the practice to be banned. Hodening was, however, benevolent, and intended to bring good fortune, the revellers singing and ringing handbells*, as they requested gifts of food, drink or money. It still survives in parts of East Kent. (See **Richmond Poor Aud 'Oss**)

Hogmanay A word of obscure origin for the last day of the year, now used to describe the New Year's Eve festival so important in Scotland, where in earlier times Christmas was little celebrated because of strong Puritan* influence. Hogmanay is essentially a time for the gathering of the clans, in the sense of cheerful family reunions, with plenty of eating, drinking and making merry. It is especially important for Scots in exile, who may manage to attend a party where tartans and bagpipes provide a nostalgic atmosphere.

Letting in the New Year is the climax of Hogmanay, and First Footing* is particularly important in Scotland, where in some parts the First Foot is not supposed to speak until he has placed peat or coal on the fire. The tokens of prosperity for the coming year include whisky, and in the East Coast fishing villages a red herring. In the old days even farm animals were given an extra feed at New Year, as we learn from Burns's poem, 'The Auld Farmer's Address to his Mare'. There are picturesque Scottish survivals of ancient new year ceremonies, such as the procession of flambeaux or torches at Comrie, Perth, the great bonfires of Wick and their accompaniment of torchlit processions and dancing*, and the Hogmanay fireballs of Stonehaven – cages of wire-netting containing rags soaked in paraffin, set alight and swung round by young men, originally to ward off evil spirits. At Biggar in Lanarkshire, an enormous bonfire accompanied by fireworks, church bells and revelry is used to burn the old year out.

Another ancient fire-ritual takes place on Old New Year's Eve (11 January) at the north-eastern Scottish seaport of Burghead, Morayshire. It is known as Burning the Clavie*, and it is claimed that it dates back to Celtic or at least to Norse times. The Clavie is a tar barrel, sawn in half and fastened by a specially forged iron on a 2-metre fisherman's pole called a spoke. A stone must be used to hammer it into position, and a fire-brand is used to light the contents of tar, wood and peat. The whole ceremony must be conducted by a hereditary group, and no stranger is allowed to help. The blazing Clavie is carried through the streets, then to the top of Doorie Hill where it is hacked to pieces by the Clavie King and his men.

No Hogmanay would be complete, of course, without an authentic singing of *Auld Lang Syne**, the world-famous song by Robert Burns, though Burns Night itself, with the traditional piping-in of the haggis, does not occur until 25 January. (See **New Year, Up-Helly-Aa**)

Holland The Dutch, more than any other nation, have maintained a strong tradition concerning St Nicholas*, whom as *Sinter Klaas* Dutch settlers took to seventeenth-century America, from where he was reintroduced into Europe as Santa Claus*. In Holland St Nicholas visits children* on 5 December, the eve of his feast day or on St Nicholas' Day itself, and he sometimes arrives by boat. He is still dressed as a bishop, with crook and mitre, riding on a white horse, preserving the link with the original Nicholas who was Bishop of Myra in the fourth century. In Dutch primary schools St Nicholas, accompanied by his assistant, the Moorish-looking *Zwarte Piet* (Black Peter), solemnly listens to a report on the behaviour of each child before he hands out his presents. Christmas in the Netherlands extends from the visit by St Nicholas until *Dreikonigen* (Epiphany*). Food specialities include *kerstol*, a kind of Christmas cake*.

Holly With its attractively-shaped leaves of dark and glossy green, and its bright berries of contrasting red, the holly (*Ilex aquifolium*) has been one of the most popular midwinter decorations* since at least the time of the Romans*, who used it during their festival of Saturnalia*. In addition to its reminder of continuing life (see **Evergreens**) there was also a sexual symbolism in holly which explains its frequent association with ivy*, the female element.

When Christians took over the old festival of Saturnalia, instead of rejecting the use of holly as a pagan custom (c.f. the non-use of mistletoe* in churches) they saw in it a vivid Christian symbolism. The white flowers of the holly reminded them of the purity of Mary*, the berries recalled the blood shed by Jesus* to redeem humankind, the prickles were a reminder of his crown of thorns. (*Kristdorn*, Christ's-thorn, is the Scandinavian word for holly.) There is a legend that the berries, which only form on female bushes, were originally white, but when the crown of thorns was pressed onto the brow of Jesus they remained for ever coloured by his blood. Even the bitter-tasting bark of the holly was seen as a symbol of the suffering of Jesus on the cross, all this well illustrated in the old carol. (See **The holly and the ivy**) Various customs involve holly, such as the ceremonial cutting at Haworth, West Yorkshire, known as 'Holly Scroggling'. (See **Holming Day**)

78

In addition to its use for Christmas decoration – round picture frames, in wreaths on doors or as a sprig on Christmas Pudding* etc. – holly has long been regarded as possessing healing properties. The berries, leaves and bark have been used to make infusions such as 'holly tea', the drinking of which was said to cure all kinds of ills. Holly picked on Christmas Day was regarded as especially potent, but when evergreen decorations were removed from the home after Twelfth Night* it was essential not to burn holly, as this was certain to bring bad luck – a superstition probably arising from the fact that holly burns with alarming crackles and detonations.

The holly and the ivy One of the oldest and best-known of English carols*, first noted in 1710, but going back to remote times, when pagan decoration was given Christian symbolism, each part of the holly being used as a reminder. For example:

> The Holly bears a berry
> As red as any blood,
> And Mary bore sweet Jesus Christ
> To do poor sinners good.   (See **Holly, Ivy**)

Holming Day A name for St Stephen's Day* (26 December) in the parts of Wales where men and boys beat each other on this day with branches of holly*, until they drew blood. Fortunately this tradition died out around the middle of the nineteenth century.

Holy Innocents The name given to the children* of Bethlehem* and the surrounding district – two years of age and under – who were massacred on the orders of Herod* in an attempt to kill the Christ-child (Matthew 2.16-18). The horror and pathos of this event is well expressed in the famous Coventry Carol*, with its reference to 'Herod the King, in his raging' and is remembered by the Church on Holy Innocents' Day (28 December), the final day in the reign of the Boy Bishop*. (**See Coventry Carol, Herod**)

Horsley, John Calcott (1817-1903) The artist who designed the first commercially produced Christmas card in 1843 at the request of Henry Cole*. He was later elected a member of the Royal Academy. (See **Christmas Cards**)

Hunting the Wren (See **Wren**)

Huron Carol A Canadian carol, remarkable in that it was originally in the language of the American Indian tribe of the Hurons. *Jesous Ahatonhia* is attributed to the martyred Jesuit missionary, Jean de Brébeuf (1593-1649).

Il est né, le divin Enfant! French carol* dating from at least the eighteenth century, evoking the shepherds* playing their *haut-bois* (oboes) and *musettes* (a kind of bagpipes). It begins:

> He is born, the Child from Heaven!
> Let the merry pipes proclaim it!
> He is born the Child from Heaven,
> Let us sing the Saviour's birth!

Immanuel Sometimes spelt 'Emmanuel', this is a Hebrew name meaning: 'With us (is) God'. It was first used as a description of the promised Messiah* by the prophet Isaiah* (7.14), who gives this as the name of the Virgin's son – a passage quoted in Matthew's account of the nativity* (Matthew 1.23) The name is used in several Christmas carols*; for example, 'Hark! The herald' includes the phrase 'Jesus, our Immanuel', and it is the last word in 'O little town of Bethlehem'. (See **Incarnation**)

In Dulci Jubilo An old German* carol*, said to have been written by the German mystic Heinrich Seure (1295-1366) following a vision of dancing* with angels*. In 1853 it was translated by John Mason Neale, beginning 'Good Christian men, rejoice!' More modern versions now appear as 'Good Christians all' or, in the USA*, 'Good Christian folk'.

In the bleak midwinter A poem written by Christina Rossetti in 1872, based on the unlikely assumption that Jesus* was born in the midst of frost, ice and deep snow. As a carol* it is usually sung to the tune 'Cranham', written for it in 1906 by Gustav Holst, and also to the setting by Harold Darke.

Incarnation The Christian doctrine that when Jesus* was born God entered human history, living on earth as human flesh and blood – hence the derivation of the term from the Latin *carnis* (flesh). The most familiar reference to the incarnation is in the prologue of St John's Gospel: 'And the Word was made flesh, and dwelt among us, and we beheld his glory, the glory as of the only begotten of the Father, full of grace and truth' (John 1.14, AV). There have been various interpretations of the nature of Christ*, ranging from those who have argued that he was merely a remarkable human being to those, like the Gnostics, who emphasized his deity to such an extent that they denied that he was really human, and thought of him as a supernatural spirit. The orthodox teaching, however, is that Jesus was both completely man and completely God, inheriting human flesh from Mary*, who conceived by the direct action of the Holy Spirit.

The incarnation is the event which has always been the central theme of Christmas. The carols*, for example, do not celebrate the birth of a great teacher and leader, but proclaim the arrival of the Saviour of humankind, who was – in the Christian view – nothing less than God stepping out onto the stage of history, the 'Word of the Father now in flesh appearing' (from 'O come all ye faithful'*). The doctrine of the incarnation is very familiar through such carols as this, and Charles Wesley's 'Hark! The herald angels sing'*, with the words:

> Veiled in flesh in Godhead see;
> Hail the incarnate Deity!

Or in less theological language, the idea is expressed in the children's* carol, 'Once in royal David's city'*:

> He came down to earth from heaven
> Who is God and Lord of all,
> And his shelter was a stable,
> And his cradle was a stall. (See also **Immanuel, Virgin Birth**)

Irving, Washington (1783-1859) American author who, even earlier than Charles Dickens*, helped to promote the keeping of Christmas, especially as a romanticized revival of earlier times. This is especially seen in his *Knickerbocker's History of New York* (1809), *Sketch Book* (1818) and *Bracebridge Hall* (1822). Irving's home, Sleepy Hollow, Terrytown, New York State, is open to the public each year to celebrate the traditional Christmas.

Isaiah The Old Testament prophet who lived in the eighth century BC and spoke of the coming of the Messiah. Many of his famous messianic prophecies are familiar through their inclusion in the Festival of Nine Lessons and Carols* and the Christmas section of Handel's *Messiah**. In particular, there are the familiar lines from the Authorized Version of the Bible: 'The people that walked in darkness have seen a great light. They that dwell in the land of the shadow of death, upon them hath the light shined ... for unto us a child is born, unto us a son is given, and the government shall be upon his shoulder, and his name shall be called Wonderful Counsellor, the Mighty God, the Everlasting Father, the Prince of Peace' (Isaiah 9.2-6) (See **Messiah, Oratorio**).

Italy The essential Italian contribution to Christmas was provided by St Francis* in 1223, when he popularized both the singing of carols* to folk tunes and the setting up of a *presepio* or nativity scene*. The most famous Italian crib* today is probably the one in the church of Santa Maria in Ara Coeli in Rome, whose seventh-century *bambino**, or infant Jesus, is said to have been carved from olive wood brought from the Garden of Gethsemane. Each Christmas children* stand before the *bambino*, reciting poems on the nativity*, and on Twelfth Night* it is carried to the top of the Capitoline Hill to bless the city of Rome.

The season begins when the *Zampognari** come to play their traditional bagpipes. On 6 December great crowds of pilgrims flock to Bari, on the southern coast of Italy, where the bones of St Nicholas* are believed to be enshrined. Though presents are exchanged on Christmas Day*, it is especially at Twelfth Night* that the children receive their gifts, brought by a mysterious witch-like figure. (See **Befana**) Italian festive specialities include *torrone* (nougat) and a *panettone* (a kind of fruit cake).

Ivy Although used much less than holly* in modern Christmas decorations*, Ivy (*Hedera helix*) was once its inseparable companion, as is shown by the old carol 'The holly and the ivy'*. The explanation for this close association is that in ancient times the soft and shapely clinging ivy symbolized the female element, the counterpart to the virile nature of the red and prickly holly. When the two plants were used in combination they provided a symbol of love and fertility, but ivy was also a bringer of good fortune, capable of warding off the evil of witchcraft, and was associated by the Romans* with Bacchus, hence the use of ivy as a symbol by inn-keepers and wine merchants.

As in the case of both holly and mistletoe* all kinds of therapeutic powers have been attributed to ivy. Poultices for ulcers and abscesses were made from the leaves, and the berries steeped in vinegar were used in an attempt to cure fever during the Great Plague of 1665. The concoction was also supposed to remove corns, and a wreath of ivy was sometimes worn on the head in the vain hope that it would prevent or cure baldness.

Ivy was sometimes used for prognostication during the Twelve Days of Christmas*. A leaf was placed in a dish of water on New Year's Eve, and left until Twelfth Night* when its state would tell the future of the person who had placed it there. Black spots near the pointed end meant disease in the feet or legs; in the middle they meant disease in the stomach, near the stalk disease in the head or neck. An unspoilt green meant good health in the coming year.

Jack Frost A personification of very cold weather, often associated with Christmas and the New Year*, though it does not seem to have been used before the nineteenth century. The French equivalent is *le Bonhomme Hiver*, and in Scandinavia* he is known as 'King Frost'.

Jack Horner One of the best-known nursery rhymes, the story of Jack Horner who helped himself to the contents of a Christmas pie probably has a basis in history. It is said that Horner was steward to the Abbot of Glastonbury during the period when Henry VIII was busy with his dissolution of the monasteries. In an attempt to influence the king the abbot is said to have sent him a handsome Christmas pie carried to London by Jack Horner. On the way Horner is supposed to have opened the pie, found that it contained the deeds of 12 manors in Somerset, including the manor of Mells, the 'plum' which he extracted for himself, and which the Horner family still possesses. (See **Christmas Pie**)

Japan Although Japanese society is permeated by Shintoism and Buddhism, the Christian celebration of Christmas is familiar to most. It is, however, largely a matter of present-giving, with the legendary old man, *Hoteiosho*, as the equivalent of Father Christmas*, and festive displays in stores, similar to those in the West. A more serious interest in the Christian tradition is shown by the existence of a Christmas Museum in Japan. (See **Christmas Archives**)

Jesse Tree Named after Jesse, the father of David, and therefore the ancestor of Jesus*, this is a representation of a tree, with branches showing it as a 'family tree' of Jesus. Some Jesse trees can be seen in stained-glass windows, as in the cathedrals of Wells and Chartres. In recent years they have been revived as decorations for Advent*, especially in the USA*. Note the old carol, 'The Noble Stem of Jesse hath flow'red on this tide'. (See **Es ist ein' Ros' entsprungen**)

Jesus Many of those who ostensibly celebrate the birth of Jesus know little or nothing about his life or teachings. His unique position amongst the figures of world history, however, is acknowledged by the fact that when he was born he divided history into two, until recently described as BC ('before Christ') and AD (*Anno Domini* – 'the year of Our Lord'). It is true that there are other calendars, such as the Jewish and Muslim, and it is also true that the Christian calendar is inaccurate. (See **Christmas Day**) But numbering the year by its distance from the approximate birth of Jesus is now universally accepted, even by governments opposed to Christianity, although it is now more common to speak of 2006 AD as '2006 CE' (Common Era), with BC dates given as 'BCE'.

The greatness of Jesus is incontestable, and more has been said and written about him than anyone else in the world. There is certainly no other person whose birth is celebrated in any way comparable to the festival of Christmas.

Although attempts have been made to show that he was not a historical figure, there is no doubt amongst scholars that the four Gospels present a person who existed in history, and that the rest of the New Testament is convincing evidence that his followers believed him to be not only a unique ethical teacher, preacher and healer, but the promised Messiah*, the Son of God (see **Incarnation**) and the Saviour of all humankind, not merely of his fellow-Jews. His name is the Greek form of Joshua (meaning 'the Lord saves') given to him by Joseph, who was told 'you are to name him Jesus, for he will save his people from their sins' (Matthew 1.21). The belief that Jesus came to save men from sin and death – especially associated with his crucifixion on Good Friday and his resurrection on Easter Sunday – is very prominent in many Christmas carols*, (e.g. 'Now ye need not fear the grave', in 'Good Christian men rejoice').

According to the Gospels of Matthew and Luke, Jesus was born in Bethlehem* in the miraculous yet lowly circumstances remembered each Christmas. Jesus then grew up in the northern part of Palestine, near the Sea of Galilee, living in the village of Nazareth with his mother Mary*, and with Joseph*, whose trade as a carpenter he followed. Only one incident is recorded concerning his childhood: his mature discussion of religious questions with the scribes in the Temple of Jerusalem (Luke 2.41-52).

At the age of about 30 Jesus began to visit the northern towns and villages of Palestine, preaching that people should repent and believe the gospel (good news) that God is a loving Father. His immense popularity came mainly from his reputation as a healer, and few at first accepted his challenging teaching. During a visit to Jerusalem, when he was about 33, Jesus was betrayed by one of his twelve disciples, hastily tried by the Jewish authorities, who condemned him to death for blasphemy, and was then crucified by the Romans* because he was also accused of treason. Within a few weeks of his death his disciple Peter and the other eleven were preaching that Jesus had been raised from the dead and was alive for evermore. The chief persecutor of Christians, Saul of Tarsus, was dramatically converted and, as the apostle Paul, began to spread the message of the risen Christ* throughout the Roman Empire. In Paul's letters and in the Acts of the Apostles the events of Good Friday and Easter Sunday are constantly stressed, but there is no emphasis on the birth of Jesus, which is regarded simply as the beginning of his work of revelation and salvation, e.g. 'Christ Jesus came into the world to save sinners' (1 Timothy 1.15). (See **Church of the Holy Nativity, Virgin Birth**)

Jingle Bells An American Christmas song, rather than a carol*, as it has no religious content. It was written for the children of a New York Sunday school by J.L. Pierpoint in 1857, and entitled 'One-Horse Open Sleigh'.

Joseph Named after the famous Joseph of the Old Testament, he was a pious carpenter who lived in the village of Nazareth in the northern Palestinian province of Galilee. Although both the Gospels of Matthew and Luke stress that he was not the father of Jesus* and that his wife Mary* was already pregnant by the Holy Spirit when he married her (see **Virgin Birth**), they nevertheless give long genealogies (Matthew 1.1-16, Luke 3.23-38) intended to show that Joseph was a descendant of David. This explains why Joseph, in accordance with Roman* law and Jewish custom, had to make the 80-mile journey south to Bethlehem*, in order to be registered for the tax census in the town of his ancestor David – the town where it had been prophesied the Messiah* would be born. According to the apocryphal *Book of James* (second century) Joseph was much older than Mary, a tradition preserved in the 'Cherry Tree Carol'* ('Joseph was an old man'). It also seems likely that he died some time before the crucifixion, because he is not mentioned in the later parts of any Gospel, and on the cross Jesus asks John to look after his mother Mary (John 19.25-27).

That Joseph was not a wealthy man is suggested not only by the fact that he had to accept a humble birthplace for Mary's son, but also by the fact that when the baby was presented at the Temple in Jerusalem he only made the poor man's sacrifice permitted in Leviticus (12.18). See Luke 2.22-24. (See **Nativity**)

Joulupukki The Finnish gift-bringer who is the equivalent of Father Christmas*, the name meaning 'Christmas Goat'. Of pagan origin, Joulupukki has been blended with St Nicholas*, and visits on Christmas Eve.

Journey of the Magi Poem by T.S. Eliot, the well-known opening lines, beginning 'A cold coming we had of it', being borrowed from a sermon preached before James I on Christmas Day 1622. (See **Nativity Sermons**)

Joy to the World Christmas hymn by Isaac Watts, sung to the tune 'Antioch', written by the American, Lowell Mason, using reminiscences of Handel's *Messiah**.

Julebuck An old Scandinavian* Christmas custom, rather like mumming, of going round the neighbourhood in disguise to bring Christmas greetings. Sometimes a man would go dressed as a bull with horns on his head, chasing revellers, a custom once practised in the Yorkshire Dales.

Julklapp A Christmas parcel with many wrappings containing a present hidden deep inside. It is brought to the house in parts of Germany* and Scandinavia* by an old man and an old woman, both wearing masks. Sometimes the parcel is thrown in through the doorway, and then the anonymous donor disappears, perhaps an association with St Nicholas*.

Kalends The Roman* festival of *Kaldendae,* lasting three days and heralding the New Year*, closely following Saturnalia*, whose boisterous atmosphere it maintained. Men dressed up in animal skins and blackened their faces (see **Mummers**) and, as at Saturnalia, evergreens* were used for decoration*. The festival of Kalends was said to be presided over by the goddesses Strenia, from whose sacred groves greenery was taken, and in whose name New Year* presents, were given. (See **France**)

Kaspar Also written 'Caspar' and 'Gaspar', this is the traditional name of the second Wise Man, who is said to have brought the gift of frankincense*. (See **Wise Men**)

King's College Chapel The Chapel of King's College, Cambridge, named after Henry VI who founded it in 1441, is famous both for the beauty of its architecture and the musical perfection of its annual Festival of Nine Lessons and Carols, first performed in 1918. One of the great treasures of King's College, always seen in the televised carol service, is the painting *The Adoration of the Magi* (1634) by Rubens. (See **Festival of Nine Lessons and Carols**)

Kissing Bough An early important English Christmas decoration*, usually the principal one in the home, before the Christmas tree* gradually took its place in the second half of the nineteenth century. It was really an elaborate setting for the bunch of mistletoe, which was its principal component, and underneath which friends and loved-ones – especially unmarried girls – were kissed, in order to ensure good fortune in general and prosperity in love, and marriage in particular. The kissing bough consisted of either a hemisphere or a complete globe made from boughs which were covered with garlands of intertwined evergreens such as holly*, laurel*, ivy* and rosemary*. On the outer horizontal rim were candles. Suspended from the top was an orange*, apple* or perhaps a golden 'witch's ball'. Round this central fruit or ball were suspended four red apples, which were said to represent the two solstices and two equinoxes. The bunch of mistletoe was suspended from the centre or attached to the bottom of the Kissing Bough. This was so important that the whole decoration was sometimes referred to as the 'mistletoe bough', a term which would otherwise be misleading, as mistletoe never grows into anything as substantial as the bough of a tree. (See **Mistletoe**)

Knecht Ruprecht Literally meaning 'the Servant Rupert' this was a character in a seventeenth-century German* play who became a Christmas gift-bringer, either replacing St Nicholas* (Santa Claus*), or acting as his assistant. He is usually a sinister figure, dressed in animal skins, and carries a stick to beat naughty children*.

Knickerbockers A group taking its name from the book by Washington Irving, who campaigned for an American-style Christmas, with an emphasis on Santa Claus, regarded as a Protestant New York tradition. It included, as well as Irving, the novelist Fenimore Cooper and Clement C. Moore, who wrote the poem 'A Visit from St Nicholas'. (See **Santa Claus**)

Krampus Sometimes written Grampus, this is a legendary figure in Central Europe and parts of Germany* who accompanies Saint Nicolas*, and threatens naughty children with his rod and whip. (See **Knecht Ruprecht**)

Kris Kringle Name used in America for a Christmas gift-bringer or Santa Claus*, derived from the German-speaking settlers' term *Christkindlein* (little Christ-child).

WASSAIL
BOWL.

Lambswool A hot and very rich Christmas drink, traditionally associated with the wassail bowl*. It is made from heated ale, sugar, eggs, cream and spices into which are tossed roasted apples* and small pieces of toast. As Robert Herrick (1591-1674) wrote:

> Now crowne the bowle full
> With gentle lamb's wool;
> Add sugar, nutmeg and ginger ...

The custom of serving Lambswool is still practised in some English inns, especially in certain parts of London, where the brew is first sampled by the City Ale Conners, who in past years appointed to check and ensure the quality of ale served. When they are satisfied they then ceremonially hoist an 'ale garland' as a signal that the assembled company may drink.

Lapland (See **Finland**)

Las Posadas A tradition in Latin American countries and in the south west of the USA* of re-enacting the journey of Mary* and Joseph* to Bethlehem*, and their eventually finding accommodation. What is now a religious fiesta appears to have originated in the *Novena* (nine days of prayer before Christmas) devised by Ignatius Loyola in the sixteenth century. (See **Mexico**)

Laurel (See **Bay**)

Lord of Misrule A kind of master of ceremonies who presided over the Christmas revelry, which once used to last until Twelfth Night*. He appears to have originated in the mock king or *Magister Ludorum* (Master of Games), who was elected during the Roman* festival of Saturnalia*, a tradition which survived in the mock religious ceremonies of the Middle Ages, such as the Feast of Fools, when a person was chosen to act as a temporary pope, king, or Boy Bishop. The Lord of Misrule was appointed by the monarch from the reign of Edward IV, and was especially popular in England during the Tudor period. Though Henry VIII was opposed to any religious burlesque, he lavished great sums of money on lively Christmas parties and banquets organized by a well-paid Lord of Misrule or 'Master of Merry Disports'.

In 1583 Stubbs complained in the *Anatomy of Abuses* of the row made by the Lord's procession of 'pypers pyping, their drummers thundering, their stumpes dancing, their belles jyngling ... like madde men'. The tradition was carried on well into the seventeenth century, particularly by the Inns of Court and by the students of Oxford and Cambridge, where a Christmas Prince was elected to arrange a variety of entertainments, including serious plays in Latin as well as English, and the boar's head feast*. (See also **Abbot of Unreason, Boy Bishop**)

97

Lucia, Queen (See **Queen of Light**)

Lucky Bod (See **New Year**)

Luther, Martin (1483-1546) Although the famous leader of the Protestant Reformation was generally opposed to church ritual, and to the veneration of the relics of the Wise Men* in Cologne Cathedral, he was a champion of the keeping of Christmas, as is shown in his sermons on the nativity*, his encouragement of the use of Christmas trees* and in his Christmas hymns. He did not, as is sometimes claimed, write 'Away in a manger'*, but he wrote, for example, the words and music of *'Vom Himmel Hoch'* for a children's* Christmas Eve pageant, the tune being later used in Bach's *Christmas Oratorio*.

Madonna This term for the Virgin Mary comes from the Italian *ma donna*, meaning 'my Lady'. It is used especially for paintings or sculptures of Mary with Jesus* as a baby or young boy. There are many very famous pictures of the Madonna and Child, especially by the great artists of the Italian Renaissance, which in recent years have been used on Christmas cards* and postage stamps*. (See **Mary**)

Magi The term used in St Matthew's Gospel (*magoi* in Greek), to describe certain visitors to the Christ-child, has been translated 'wise men' in most versions, but in some contemporary versions as 'astrologers'. This is misleading, because the Magi were also priests and men of considerable status, otherwise they would not have had such easy access to Herod*. The term has no real equivalent in English (the French simply call them *les Trois Mages*), but is the plural of the term *magus*, which was used to describe high-caste Zoroastrian priests from ancient Persia – revered sages who studied the heavens and had a tradition of a coming messiah. (See **King's College Chapel**, **Wise Men**)

Magnificat The hymn of praise sung by Mary* after she had become pregnant (Luke 1.46-56), so called after the opening words in Latin, *Magnificat anima mea dominum* ('My soul doth magnify the Lord'). Like the Ave Maria* it has been used as a prayer since the early days of the Church and has been set to music by many great composers, notably Bach, in his *Magnificat in D*.

Mak the Sheep stealer (See **Mystery Plays**)

Manger Derived from the French *manger* (to eat), this is an old word for a box or trough containing hay or other food for cattle etc. It is referred to three times by St Luke, who tells us that Mary* placed her baby in a manger instead of a normal cradle, implying that the birth took place in some kind of stable. (See **Nativity**) The manger is now frequently represented by a model crib* containing a doll. Five wooden slats claimed to be from the actual manger are kept as relics in the Church of Santa Maria Maggiore, Rome. A Bethlehem* stable or cattle shed was usually part of the house, especially a cave or cellar underneath, not an isolated wooden shed as is often depicted on Christmas cards.

Mari Lwyd A curious Welsh custom practised during the Christmas season, known in English as Grey Mare or Grey Mary, the latter being the meaning of the Welsh, *Mari Llwyd* (pronounced 'hloo-id'). It has affinities with both the antics of mummers* and wassailing*, and almost certainly dates from prehistoric rituals connected with the winter solstice*. The Mari Lwyd is the skull of a horse, decorated with ribbons and furnished with glass eyes, fastened on top of a pole which is carried round by a man covered by a white sheet – rather like a person in a pantomime horse. Traditionally the Mari Lwyd is led through the streets by a group playing roles, such as 'Leader', 'Sergeant', 'Corporal', 'Ostler', 'Betsie', 'Merryman' (traditionally a fiddler) and 'Punch and Judy'. They stop outside a house, singing verses and asking permission to enter. The householder and his friends sing verses in reply, and the Mari Lwyd party is invited into the house for Christmas food* and drink. To refuse the Mari Lwyd is extremely unlucky. The lower jaw of the skull is moveable, and the horse is sometimes made to snap at passers-by, who are only released if they pay a forfeit.

The custom used to be widely practised in Wales, but now survives mainly in a few South Wales valleys, such as at Llantrisant in Glamorganshire. An English equivalent of Mari Lwyd – also involving the skull of a horse – used to be common in the last century. (See **Hodening**)

Marrons glacés (See **Chestnuts**)

Mary The mother of Jesus* is known to us by the Greek version of her name, 'Mary', which is the equivalent of the Hebrew 'Miriam'. Apart from the annunciation*, the Magnificat* and the account of the nativity given by St Matthew and St Luke, we learn very little about Mary in the Gospels, other than that she was the wife of Joseph*, a carpenter who lived in Nazareth. Though both Matthew and Luke say that Mary was already pregnant by the

Holy Spirit, only Matthew mentions 'the angel* of the Lord' telling Joseph not to be afraid to marry her (Matthew 1.18-20). There are occasional references to Mary during the lifetime of Jesus, such as her concern when he was missing as a boy of twelve (Luke 2.41-52) and her fear that he was overexerting himself (Mark 3.21, 31), but Mary remains very much in the background.

By the time of the crucifixion she appears to have become a widow, as there is no mention of Joseph in the later parts of the Gospels, and we are told that Jesus speaks words of comfort to his mother from the cross, asking his disciple John to take care of her (John 19.25-27). Later, Mary is mentioned as one of those present in the upper room in Jerusalem when the Church was first organized.

Christians of all denominations have always honoured Mary as the humble girl who was privileged to become the mother of Jesus. Roman Catholics regard her as a person to be venerated, and pray to her as the Blessed Virgin Mary, Mother of God, especially in the 'Hail, Mary' or 'Ave, Maria'* and in 'The Litany of Our Lady'. The doctrine that she was not only a perpetual virgin but was entirely free from sin, the dogma of the Immaculate Conception, was formally proclaimed in 1854, and the dogma of her bodily Assumption into heaven in 1950.

Many of the carols* refer to the fact, mentioned by both Matthew and Luke and stated in both the Apostles' Creed and the Nicene Creed, that Mary was a virgin when she gave birth to Jesus. (See **Nativity** and **Virgin Birth**)

Mary's Boy Child   West Indian Christmas song by Jester Hairston, first recorded by Harry Belafonte in 1956, and top of the charts for six successive weeks around Christmas 1957.

Marzipan   Originally known in England as 'marchpane' (from Italian *marzapane),* this is a mixture of ground almonds, egg-white and sugar. Almonds were brought from the Middle East at least as early as Tudor times, and soon became a favourite Christmas delicacy in the form of marchpane sweetmeats and a rich covering for the Twelfth Cake*, which, in the form of the modern Christmas cake*, uses the majority of marzipan produced today.

Mead   One of the oldest of alcoholic drinks popular at Christmas-time, mead is made from fermented honey. Sometimes spices are added, when it is heated to make a mulled drink.

Melchior   Traditional name of the first of the three Wise Men, who brought a gift of gold*. Said to be the oldest of the three and an Arabian king, his gift was a symbol of royalty. (See **Wise Men**)

100

Merry Christmas or **Happy Christmas** The traditional greeting so familiar in English has an equivalent in most languages of the world. Here are some of the commonest: *Joyeux Noël!* (French), *Fröhliche Weihnachten!* (German), *Feliz Navidad!* (Spanish), *Boas Festas!* (Portuguese), *Buon Natale!* (Italian), *Kala Christouyenna!* (Greek), *God Jul!* (Norwegian and Swedish), *Glaedelig Jul!* (Danish), *Vrolijk Keerstfeest!* (Dutch), *Christos Rozdajestja!* (Russian), *Sarbatori Vesele!* (Romanian), *Srecan Bozic!* (Croatian), *Goze Narodzenie!* (Polish), *Vesele Vanoce!* (Czech), *Srozhdestvom Kristovym!* (Ukranian), *Hauskaa Joulua!* (Finnish*)*, *Nadolig Llawen!* (Welsh), *Kung He Xin Xi!* (Chinese), *Kurisumasu Omedeto!* (Japanese).

Messiah A Hebrew word, meaning 'one who is anointed' (i.e. by God). It is a title given by Christians to Jesus*, usually in the form of 'Christ'*, the Greek translation of *Messiah*. Originally, the rite of anointing – the placing of holy oil on the head – was the Hebrew way of consecrating a king, as in the case of Saul and David. Later the Old Testament prophets foretold the coming of a descendant of King David, who would be specially anointed by God to save his people and usher in a kingdom of righteousness as the Prince of Peace (Isaiah 7.13, 14; 9.1-7 etc.). He would also be the Suffering Servant, who would die to redeem mankind (Isaiah 53) and would be born in David's native town of Bethlehem* (Micah 5.2-5).

The term 'Messiah' is well known through its use as the title of Handel's great oratorio (often incorrectly called 'The *Messiah*'), the first part of which deals with the messianic prophecies and the birth of Christ. It has become traditional to perform at least this first section of Handel's *Messiah* every Christmas, both on the radio and in concert halls and churches. (See **Handel's Messiah**)

Mexico Celebrated in Mexico since the sixteenth century, Christmas begins on the 12 December with a fiesta in the home of the patron saint of Mexico, the Virgin of Guadeloupe, who is said to have miraculously appeared in 1531. The Mexican form of *Las Posadas* is a night-time procession in which children* carry images of Mary* and Joseph* to a place of lodging where they are finally admitted. In the city of Oaxaca there is the tradition of the *Noche del Rabano* (23 December), during which huge radishes are carved into characters in the story of the nativity*. All over the country Christmas is celebrated by brightly costumed dancers, some performing traditional dramas such as *Los matachines*, portraying the conflict between the Moors and Christians in Spain*, and *Las Pastorelas*, telling the story of the shepherds*.

After Midnight Mass, *La Misa de Gallo,* many Mexicans have their special meal, which usually includes turkey*, appropriately so, as this is where the birds were first captured and taken to Europe. (See **Poinsettia**)

Midnight Mass The Midnight Mass, the popular name for the first Mass of Christmas, is particularly important in Catholic countries, and in France*, for example, it has long been the custom to begin the festivities on returning home from *la Messe de Minuit*. Protestants have increasingly adopted the custom so that attendance at Midnight Communion on Christmas Eve is now popular in England, and some form of eucharistic service usually appears on television.

Milly Box A small box, such as a shoe-box, carried round by children* in quest of a Christmas gift. In the box was a doll representing the Virgin Mary* and/or the Baby Jesus*. 'Milly' is derived from 'My Lady'. The centuries-old custom of taking a box from house to house survived in northern England until the early years of the twentieth century.

Mince Pies One of the oldest established traditional Christmas foods*, mince pies are so called because the pastry case is filled with mincemeat, which was originally just what the name suggests – minced meat, especially mutton; minced, it has been said, to help the many people in past years who had badly decayed teeth and toothless gums. From Tudor times until the late eighteenth century, the pies varied a good deal in content, and sometimes contained an expensive mixture of minced or chopped game, poultry and wild birds – tongue, rabbit, goose*, duck, chicken, turkey*, pigeon, partridge, curlews, blackbirds, snipe, woodcock etc.

The more ordinary pies were mostly filled with minced or shredded mutton, which was mixed with dried fruit*, dates and spices* – the latter probably added

as a reminder of the Wise Men* from the East – though spices also helped to mask the flavour of meat that was no longer fresh. Because the fruit mixture (flavoured with brandy*, which also acted as a preservative) could be prepared in advance of Christmas, unlike the meat that was added last, the fruit content gradually took over until the pies were entirely sweet. The typical modern mincemeat now consists of raisins, currants, sultanas, candied peel, apples*, and spices, with suet as the only reminder of its early meat content.

Mince pies were originally oval or oblong, designed as a reminder of the manger-cradle or crib*, and they were sometimes topped with a pastry figure, cut out in the form of the Christ-child. An old tradition was to eat a mince pie on each of the Twelve Days of Christmas* in order to ensure twelve happy months in the coming year. As each pie was eaten it was the custom to wish the person consuming it 'Happy Month!'. Many British families still make their own mince pies, along with Christmas cake* and pudding*.

Mistletoe Along with holly* the best known of the traditional Christmas decorations*, though entirely pagan in its original use. Mistletoe (*Viscum album*) derives its botanical name from the Latin *albus* meaning 'white', referring to the translucent white berries, and from *viscus* meaning 'sticky', referring to the substance secreted by the berries. This substance was regarded as of great medicinal value and gave the mistletoe its other name, All Heal*. Mistletoe, sometimes referred to as the 'Golden Bough', was sacred to both the Druids* and the Scandinavians* who regarded it as divine, because of its unusual appearance and because it grew without touching the earth. It is, in fact, a parasitic plant whose seeds are deposited in crevices in tree trunks by birds taking the berries, hence the name mistle thrush. Although in ancient times it was considered especially sacred when growing on an oak, mistletoe grows mostly on apple* trees, and anyone travelling through Normandy, for example, will notice that it is commercially grown in the orchards of northern France*. Rarely cultivated in Britain, it grew here naturally. The oldest surviving market for mistletoe and holly is held at Tenbury Wells in Herefordshire.

The Celtic custom which links mistletoe with Christmas was the ceremonial cutting by the Druids at the time of the winter solstice*. Pliny describes in his *Historia Naturalis* (c. 77 AD) how these white-robed priests severed the mistletoe with a golden sickle. It was caught in a white sheet held by virgins, so that it was not polluted by touching the base earth. Then two white bulls were slaughtered, and the mistletoe was distributed among the people, who hung it up to protect their homes.

The Scandinavians considered the plant sacred because of the Norse legend concerning the sun god, Baldur the Beautiful. The evil god Loki discovered that Baldur was divinely invulnerable to arrows made from any wood except mistletoe, which had been thought too weak to be used for such a purpose. Loki took a piece of mistletoe, made an arrow with it and put it into a bow held by the blind god Hoder, who accidentally killed Baldur with the arrow. Baldur was restored to life, ever after bringing health and prosperity.

Mistletoe was also a symbol of fertility, and it is this aspect, combined with its role as a bringer of peace and good fortune, that is the origin of the ancient English custom of kissing under the mistletoe. Surprised comments recorded by early European visitors show that England was the only country to have this custom at the time. One version of the tradition is that a man was entitled to as many kisses as there were berries on the mistletoe. He was also supposed to pluck a berry after each kiss and try to reach the ideal number of ten to ensure good fortune. So the idea was to get to the mistletoe early, while there were still berries to pluck! Later it became essential to burn the mistletoe after Twelfth Night* to ensure that its magic spell to procure love and marriage would not be broken.

Because of its pagan associations Mistletoe was traditionally not used as a Christmas decoration in the main rooms of large houses or in most churches. There was even a legend that it was the wood which had been used to make the Cross and that it was for ever cursed. However, as in the case of holly, a Christian symbolism was superimposed here and there, and it was said that the Holy Trinity was represented by the clusters of three berries which often occur on mistletoe. A remarkable exception to the general attitude about church decoration is seen in the ancient Christmas custom of using mistletoe in York Minster. (See **Kissing Bough, Pickwick Papers, York Minster**)

Molly Dancers A name, corrupted from 'My Lady Dancers', for Christmas revellers who used to be well known in the Cambridgeshire Fens. They were popular groups of musicians and costumed dancers, who visited the villages and farms, starting on Christmas Eve.

Mulled Wine A popular drink at Christmas, this is wine which has been heated – traditionally with a red-hot poker – and to which sugar and spices* have been added. The term, also used for mulled ale, cider and mead*, may be derived from the obsolete 'mulsed', from Latin *mulcere* (to sweeten). A similar Christmas drink popular in Germany*, Austria* and Switzerland is *Glühwein* (literally 'glow-wine') (See **Bishop, Mead, Punch**)

Mummers Groups of actors who perform traditional plays, especially during the Christmas season. The name is probably derived from the German* *Mumme* (mask), as the players used to wear grotesque disguises and costumes, and sometimes blackened their faces, draping these and their clothes with paper streamers or strips of parchment. Mumming is very ancient, and is believed to have originated in prehistoric fertility rituals, mainly because in the typical mummer's play a dead character is restored to life. The dressing-up may have its origins in the Roman* Kalends. The actual play varied from district to district, but a typical story opens with a short word of welcome by the narrator: 'Here comes I, old Father Christmas!'

Then it depicts the fight between St George (in later years, King George) and the dragon. When the dragon is killed, Father Christmas appeals for a doctor, who restores him to life, but he is killed by St George a second time. The hero, having won the hand of 'fair Sabra, the King of Egypt's* daughter' is challenged to a sword-fight by Bold Slasher, the Turkish knight. The knight is killed, but is restored to life by the doctor. Other characters who appeared, according to region and tradition, were Giant Turpin, Wild Work, Pickle Herring, Ginger Breeches, Allspice, Happy Jack, Beelzebub, and even the comparatively recent figures of Cromwell, Nelson and Napoleon. The play usually ended with an appeal by Father Christmas, such as:

Now ladies and gentlemen, your sport is just ended
So prepare for the box, which is highly commended;
The box it would speak if it had but a tongue
Come, throw in your money, and think it no wrong.

Mummers were still active in Victorian times, and even today a few traditional groups survive, notably in Marshfield, Gloucestershire, where the play is performed on Boxing Day*. The Marshfield Mummers are known as the Paper Boys, because they wear traditional costumes composed of many short strips of coloured paper which cover them from head to foot. They introduce themselves to the crowd, have a miraculous restoration to life by a doctor, and finally go round with the collecting-box. Mumming spread from England to wherever there were English settlers, and in Philadelphia in the USA*, for example, there is a New Year's Day procession of thousands of mummers. (See also **Hodening, Kalends, Mari Lwyd, Richmond 'Oss**)

Music Christmas music, in addition to carols*, ranges from church music to popular songs. There are, for example, settings by Bach of the *Magnificat**, his Advent cantata, *Wachet Auf!* ('Sleepers, awake!') and his *Christmas Oratorio**, Handel's *Messiah**, Corelli's Concerto Grosso, *Christmas Night,* Scarlatti's *Cantata Pastorale,* Daquin's *Noël Suisse,* settings of *Ave Maria** (Bach/Gounod and Schubert), and classical music associated with Christmas, such as Haydn's 'Christmas Symphony', 'The Toy Symphony', now attributed to Leopold Mozart, Rossini's opera *La Cenerentola,* Rimsky-Korsakov's opera *Christmas Eve,* Tchaikovsky's *Nutcracker** *Suite,* Wagner's *Siegfried Idyll,* Berlioz's *The Childhood of Christ,* Liszt's *Christmas Tree Suite,* Humperdinck's opera *Hansel and Gretel,* Adolphe Adam's song *Cantique de Noël* ('O Holy Night'), W.H. Fry's *Santa Claus Symphony,* Prokofiev's ballet *Cinderella,* Vaughan Williams's *Fantasia on Christmas Carols,* Benjamin Britten's *A Ceremony of* Carols, and appropriate short pieces, such as musical sleigh-rides by Leopold Mozart, Delius and Prokofiev. (See **Songs, Vienna**)

Myrrh Like frankincense*, this is obtained from the resin exuded by a shrub, the thorny *Commiphora myrrha,* grown in Arabia and Abyssinia. It was prized for its healing properties, and tincture of myrrh for rubbing on gums is still known to modern pharmacy. It was used as an ointment and as a soporific. When Jesus* was crucified he was offered 'wine mingled with myrrh' to deaden the pain, but refused it (Mark 15.23). Myrrh was also used by Joseph of Arimathea when he prepared the body of Jesus for the tomb (John 19.38-40). It was so expensive that it was said to have been worth more than its weight in gold. One of three gifts presented by the Wise Men*, myrrh is seen by Christians as a symbol of the suffering and death that Jesus would eventually undergo.

Mystery Plays These medieval English plays telling the story of the Fall and salvation through Christ are relevant to Christmas as they include a depiction of the nativity*. The name 'mystery' is ultimately derived from Latin *ministerium*, meaning an employment or trade, because the plays were performed by the various guilds of tradesmen such as tailors, glovers, fishmongers etc., each usually contributing a particular scene, performed in the streets on a decorated cart. They are described as 'cycles', mainly from Coventry, Chester, York and Wakefield. The latter, for example, includes comic scenes involving Mak the Sheep-stealer and dialect-speaking shepherds* who visit the new-born child in Bethlehem*, taking him simple presents of a bunch of cherries, a bird and a ball. (See **Coventry Carol**)

Nativity By the term 'the nativity' Christians mean the birth of Jesus*, celebrated at Christmas, which is 'the Feast of the Nativity'. The story of how Jesus came to be born in Bethlehem in Roman-occupied Palestine is told in the first chapters of the Gospels of St Luke and St Matthew. Although the birth is not actually described in St John's Gospel, the first chapter (or prologue) contains the famous interpretation of the meaning of the nativity, which Christians believe to be the act of God entering history and taking on human form, so that Jesus was both man and God. (See **Incarnation***)

St Luke begins his account with the story of how Mary* was visited by the angel Gabriel* in Nazareth, and explains that Joseph* travelled with his wife to Bethlehem (80 miles to the south) in order to be registered in the Roman* census which had been ordered by Caesar Augustus*. The overcrowding of the town caused by the census accounts for the fact that, although Mary's pregnancy was well-advanced, 'there was no room for them in the inn' (Luke 21-27). We are not actually told that Jesus was born in a stable, but this is implied by Luke's statement that Mary 'gave birth to her firstborn son, wrapped him in bands of cloth and laid him in a manger'*.

The kind of stable Jesus was born in would not have been the wooden structure so often imagined, but a small cavern cut out of the limestone rock underneath a house or inn, of the type still seen in Bethlehem. The cavern traditionally believed to be the birthplace was visited by St Helena, whose son Constantine – the first Christian Emperor – built over it in 330 AD the Church of the Holy Nativity, the oldest church in the world.

St Luke tells us that the birth was announced by an angel* to shepherds* who were looking after their flocks, camping out that night in the nearby fields. Their reaction to the supernatural visitation was at first one of terror, but they ran to Bethlehem 'and found Mary and Joseph, and the baby lying in a manger' (Luke 2.8-20).

St Matthew's Gospel makes no mention of the shepherds, but describes a visit to the infant Jesus made by 'wise men from the East' (Matthew 2.1). Contrary to popular belief Matthew does not say that they were kings, or even that there were three of them. These ideas arise from the fact that they were of sufficient importance to gain access to Herod* and that they presented three expensive gifts: gold*, frankincense* and myrrh.*

Note that it is only Matthew who mentions the guiding star* and that he refers to the Wise Men* arriving at a 'house', not a stable, presumably some time after the visit of the shepherds (Matthew 2.1-11). The visit of the Wise Men is officially celebrated at Epiphany* (6 January). Matthew also tells of the jealous wrath of Herod* who, in an attempt to kill the infant Jesus, orders the massacre of the Holy Innocents*. The fact that his orders are to kill children 'two years old and under' confirms that the visit of the Wise Men occurred when Jesus was no longer a tiny baby. Matthew adds that both the Wise Men and Joseph are warned in a dream of the insane jealousy of Herod and that Mary and Joseph managed to escape with the child to Egypt *(Matthew 2.12-18).

Both Luke and Matthew stress that the birth of Jesus was a supernatural event, accompanied by supernatural phenomena heralding the birth of the long-expected Messiah* (or Christ*) in the ancestral city of David. (For the probable date of the Nativity see **Christmas Day**, and **Bethlehem, Church of the Holy Nativity, Virgin Birth.**)

Nativity Light A special kind of candle*, usually in the form of a cube, with transparent coloured pictures of the nativity* on each of its four sides. When it is lit the scenes are illuminated from inside, looking like miniature stained-glass windows. It is particularly associated with Ireland, where candles are traditionally placed in windows on Christmas Eve. A Nativity Light is allowed to burn at least through Christmas Eve like a yule-candle*.

Nativity Plays Dramatizations of the events surrounding the nativity* have been performed from as early as the ninth century. In the Middle Ages the performance, especially in Italy, often centred round a permanent *presepio* or crib*, where the *bambino*, a doll representing the Christ-child, was reverently placed in the crib as part of a church service. Although the medieval nativity plays were as much rituals as dramas some of them were nevertheless realistic enough to include convincing shepherds and an *obstetrix,* or midwife, as in the York cycle of Mystery Plays*.

It is a firmly-established tradition in primary schools to perform a simple nativity play, with children* dressed as shepherds*, angels*, Three Kings, Herod*, Mary* and Joseph*, and a doll in the manger*, the most coveted role for many a little girl being that of Mary. The play usually includes music and the singing of carols*, in which the audience, mostly composed of proud parents and grandparents, can join. Nativity plays are so popular that stores report a marked pre-Christmas increase in the sale of striped tea-towels. (See **Nativity Scene**)

Nativity Scene A representation of the nativity (see above) by means of figures surrounding a doll representing the baby Jesus*, which is usually lying on straw or hay in a model of the manger*. Sometimes the term 'crib'* is used for the whole scene, though this actually refers only to the manger.

The figures are usually those of Mary* (traditionally dressed in blue) and Joseph*, with the addition of two or three shepherds* and sometimes models of cattle, sheep, a donkey and perhaps a camel. It is also customary to include three Wise Men*, dressed as kings and presenting their gifts of gold*, frankincense* and myrrh* – though St Matthew does not say that there were three, nor that they were kings, and says that they visited a house not a stable, and that the baby was no longer new-born.

The idea of setting up a nativity scene as a model may date back to 400 AD in Rome. In the eighth century there is mention of one at the fifth-century Church of Santa Maria Maggiore, which contains amongst its relics what are said to be remnants of the actual manger of Bethlehem*. The figure of the *bambino** Christ-child in the crib at the Church of Santa Maria in Ara Coeli, also in Rome, is supposed to have been carved out of wood from the Mount of Olives. The best-known nativity scene is the one set up by St Francis of Assisi* at Greccio, Northern Italy, in 1223, when he used a manger filled with straw, and real animals.

After the popularization of the nativity scene by St Francis and his friars, its use spread to Austria* and southern Germany*, especially Bamberg, where sometimes it was part of a large model of Bethlehem. In France* little figures known as *santons** were made for the *crèche* or crib, and are still popular. Nativity scenes are now common in Protestant as well as Catholic churches, and a smaller version is sometimes the Christmas centre-piece in Christian homes. In recent years large-scale nativity scenes have appeared in the windows of large stores and in the open in town centres. (See **Crib Friends**)

Nativity Sermons A series of Christmas sermons preached before James I by Bishop Lancelot Andrewes, in 1622. His Christmas Day* sermon opened with words about the Wise Men* later borrowed by T. S. Eliot, and usually assumed to have been written by him: 'A cold coming they had of it ... just the worst time of the year to take a journey ... The ways deep and the weather sharp... the very dead of winter.'

New Year The earliest festival of the year is dedicated to Janus, the Roman* god after which January is named. He had two heads, one looking back over the old year, one forward towards the new. The modern New Year's Eve falls exactly a week after Christmas Eve, and in many countries has the atmosphere of a brief revival of Christmas, with the same festive surroundings and even the same kind of food*. From time immemorial there has been at least a week of celebration around the shortest day of the winter solstice*, and Christmas merges into the New Year in the way that in Roman times Saturnalia* merged into Kalends*. The difference is that New Year's Eve is essentially a time of reminiscence and mutual good wishes for the year ahead, with less religious content than Christmas, though a certain sense of spiritual and moral values can be seen in the custom of making New Year resolutions. A Christian minority go further, and take part in the self-examination and re-dedication required by a Watchnight service.

In Scotland, and to some extent in France, there is a more lively celebration at New Year than at Christmas. In Scotland and in the north of England, and in a few other parts, the tradition of First Footing* is still maintained. The idea is that the first person to set foot in the house in the new year must fulfil certain strict conditions in order to bring good fortune to the household. If no visitor has agreed to arrive on time to perform the ceremony, a member of the assembled party goes out just before midnight on New Year's Eve. It is usually a male, as there is a widespread superstition that it is very unlucky for a woman to be the first to enter, though in the Isle of Man, the first foot, known as a *quaaltagh*, may be male or female. In certain parts of Yorkshire the first foot is known as the Lucky Bod (bird). In the small Yorkshire town of Driffield children* chase through the streets on the morning of New Year's Day, asking shopkeepers for a treat – originally pennies heated on a shovel, then scattered. In most areas the first foot has to be dark-haired and as handsome as possible. As soon as midnight has struck he 'lets in the New Year' by entering through the front door, usually carrying tokens of good fortune.

Both at Allendale in Northumberland and St Ives in Cornwall a group of men known as guisers still help to bring in the New Year. The term is derived from the disguise they wear – bright costumes and blackened faces. In Cornwall they dance in the streets, and in Northumberland, after calling at various public houses, form a procession, carrying on their heads barrels of blazing tar which they then throw onto a huge bonfire, before performing the task of first footing. Similar ancient fire rituals also survive in Scotland, as in the Burning of the Clavie*.

Other, more usual, ways of letting in the New Year are the ringing of church bells, the sounding of hooters and whistles on ships, trains etc., outdoor revelries and firework displays, and the broadcast chimes of Big Ben. The influence of Scotland is felt in family gatherings and parties all over the world, where it is traditional to see in the New Year by crossing arms and joining hands to the singing of 'Auld Lang Syne'*, the dialect phrase which Robert Burns uses for 'days long since'. (See also **Hogmanay, Up-helly-Aa, Watchnight**)

New Zealand Christmas in the antipodes lacks the atmosphere of brightening up the cold, dark days of the winter solstice, and is more likely to be spent on the beach than indoors. It has, however, been enthusiastically celebrated in New Zealand ever since 1814, when the missionary Samuel Marsden preached the first Christmas sermon. Traditional festive food* and decorations* are much like those in Britain, but there is a New Zealand kind of Christmas tree* which produces red flowers at this season, known by its Maori name of *Pohutukawa.*

Nowell An old word for Christmas, or an expression of joy at Christmas-time, familiar through the carol*, 'The first Nowell'. It is derived from the French word for Christmas, *Noël*, which in turn is derived from the Latin *natalis,* meaning 'birth'.

Nunc Dimittis (See **Candlemas**)

Nutcracker Music from the ballet by Tchaikovsky, first performed in St Petersburg, 17 December 1892. Based on a story by the German fantasy writer E.T.A. Hoffman, 'The Nutcracker and the Mouse King', the ballet concerns a girl called Clara, who is given a doll in the form of a nutcracker for Christmas. She dreams of a battle with mice, and is rescued by her prince, the Nutcracker, who takes her to his fairytale kingdom.

Nuts Along with dates, figs and so on, nuts traditionally follow the Christmas meal. The use of the nutcracker has largely given way to a great variety of ready-shelled nuts: hazels, walnuts, Brazils, peanuts, pistachios, pecan, cashew and especially almonds, which are also ground to make marzipan*. However, though used much less, the link between nutcrackers* and Christmas is preserved by the title of Tchaikovsky's ballet, popular at this season. (See above, also **Chestnuts**)

O come, all ye faithful! This is a translation of a Latin hymn dating from at least the eighteenth century, the first line of which is: *Adeste fideles laeti triumphantes*. The translation was made in 1841 by the Revd Frederick Oakley for the Margaret Street Chapel, London. The tune of 'Adeste Fideles' appeared in manuscript as early as 1751.

O little town of Bethlehem This hymn was written by the American Episcopalian minister, Phillips Brooks (1835-93) following a visit to Bethlehem* on Christmas Eve 1865, when he had first seen the town from the Shepherds' Field*. It is now mostly sung to 'Forest Green', a traditional tune collected in 1903 by R. Vaughan Williams.

O Tannenbaum! An old German song in praise of the faithfulness of the fir tree, green in the midst of winter snow, and bright with lighted candles*.

Odin Known to the Anglo Saxons* as Woden* (hence 'Wednesday', Woden's Day), Odin was one of the old gods of Scandinavia*, worshipped at the midwinter festivals which anticipated Christmas. (See **Winter Solstice** and **Yule-tide**) He is particularly interesting as a possible ancestor of Father Christmas*, though much of this tradition can be traced back to St Nicholas*, the original Santa Claus*.

In the Norse legends and sagas Odin is usually described as a very old man, tall, black-bearded, one-eyed, with a hat pulled down over his face, and wearing a blue cloak. He rides through the stormy winter sky in the *asgardereid*, or Wild Hunt, rewarding the worthy by bringing gifts, and punishing the wicked. His eight-footed horse, *Sleipnir*, was possibly the origin of the later idea that a reindeer – in one version, eight reindeer – drew the sleigh of Santa Claus through the sky. The curious custom of taking round a horse's skull (see **Hodening** and **Mari Lwyd**) may also be connected with Odin's legendary horse.

Old Christmas Day Since at least the early part of the fourth century the western Church has observed 25 December as Christmas Day*. However, in 1582 the old Julian Calendar (named after Julius Caesar) was abandoned in favour of the more accurate Gregorian Calendar. Britain did not adopt this until 1752, by which date it was 12 days behind the continental calendar. So when the change was made many people continued to think that Christmas did not actually occur until 6 January, which was known as 'Christmas Day, Old Style', or Old Christmas Day. The Ukranian Church, for example, still keeps to the Julian Calendar and celebrates Christmas around 7 January, as do Coptic and Ethiopian Christians. (See also **Epiphany, Haxey Hood Game**)

117

Old Tup   The northern custom of mummers going round during the Christmas period with a man or boy wearing a ram's head, and the group performing a little mumming play and singing the old song 'The Derby Ram'. (See **Mumming**)

Once in royal David's city   This well-known carol*, originally published as a children's hymn in 1848, is by Dublin-born Cecil Frances Alexander, wife of the Archbishop of Armagh, also the author of 'All things bright and beautiful' and 'There is a green hill far away'. It is sung to the tune 'Irby', which first appeared in 1849, later harmonized by H.J. Gauntlett. (See **Festival of Nine Lessons and Carols**)

Oranges   Though a comparatively recent inclusion, oranges make a contribution to Christmas, especially the small, sweet, often seedless varieties such as tangerines (once wrapped in silver paper), mandarins and satsumas. (See **Fruit**).

Oratorio   Named after the musical services at the Oratory of St Philip Neri in Rome, these are works for orchestra, soloists and choir, semi-dramatic in nature. The best-known oratorios heard during the Christmas season are Bach's *Christmas Oratorio** (1734), Handel's *Messiah** (1742) and Berlioz's *The Childhood of Christ* (1854).

Oysters   A well-established course at a Christmas dinner, oysters are especially popular as starters in France*, Britain and America. Barrels of Christmas oysters are mentioned by Charles Dickens*, and they were so cheap in the previous century that Samuel Johnson fed them to his cat.

Pantomime   A traditional theatrical entertainment, which usually begins immediately after Christmas Day* and, if successful, may be performed throughout January, February and even into March. As the name suggests, pantomime had its origin in actual mime performed by masked actors, possibly as far back as the Romans*, from whose Saturnalia* festival may be derived the topsy-turvy tradition of women dressing up as men (e.g. the 'principal boy') and men dressing up as women (e.g. dames and the Ugly Sisters). The beginnings of modern pantomime can be seen in the Italian entertainment known as *Commedia dell' Arte*, which reached England via France around 1717, bringing the traditional characters Polichinelle (Punchinello, the origin of Punch), Harlequin, Columbine, Scaramouche etc. Scenic effects and clowning were the chief characteristics, especially after 1758, when the famous Grimaldi family appeared in England.

118

The real turning-point occurred at Christmas 1759, when David Garrick introduced a new 'speaking pantomime' at his Drury Lane theatre. Appearing in a prologue as Mother Shipton (probably the first real 'dame'), he announced that he had at last taught his son (Harlequin) to speak, so there was to be no more mime. Further adapted by John Rich, of the Theatre Royal, Covent Garden, pantomime gradually became a musical show, with Mother Shipton, played by a man, as a kind of ugly fairy godmother, producing spectacular transformation scenes. Soon it became the norm to have a 'dame' and a 'principal boy', and in modern times pantomime has had a special appeal for children, who still delight in the traditional elements of scene transformations, extravagant costumes, vigorous clowning and audience participation.

With the exception of *Robin Hood, Dick Whittington* and *Robinson Crusoe* the subjects are all fairy-tales, the most popular of which is *Cinderella,* based on the French version of the ancient Chinese fairy-tale by Perrault, with the addition of Dandini, a character borrowed by the dramatist H.J. Byron from Rossini's operatic version of the story, *La Cenerentola.* He also added a character to the tale of *Aladdin* when he invented 'Widow Twankey', named after a type of China tea popular at the time. Other pantomime subjects are *Babes in the Wood, Jack and the Beanstalk, Mother Goose* and *Sleeping Beauty.*

Paper Hats (See **Crowns, paper**)

Paradise Tree The *Paradiesbaum,* featured in medieval plays, especially in Germany*, which retold the Genesis story of Adam and Eve and the forbidden fruit at Christmas time. Hung with apples*, it was an early form of Christmas tree*.

Peppercake Nothing to do with pepper, but named after allspice, which was commonly known as 'Jamaican Pepper'. (See **Spices**) In North and East Yorkshire this was always part of the housewife's traditional Christmas baking, often made to a local recipe.

Peppercorn Rent Paid as a single peppercorn by the town of New Castle in Pennsylvania, USA*, this arrives every Christmas Eve at Buckingham Palace, a rent paid to the Queen, first commanded by William III in 1693.

Père Fouettard In France* there is a tradition that whereas good children* receive presents at Christmas, naughty children are punished by the dark-bearded figure known as *le Père Fouettard,* whose name is derived from *le fouet* (birch rod).

Pickwick Papers *Pickwick Papers* contains one of Charles Dickens'* most delightful pictures of a Victorian Christmas. First published in serial form in

1836, the twenty-eighth chapter, 'A Good Humoured Christmas Chapter', includes an eloquent justification of this 'happy state of companionship and mutual goodwill, which is a source of such pure and unalloyed delight'. This is an account of the comical antics of the Pickwickians, the Wellers and the Fat Boy, as they spend Christmas with the Wardles at Dingley Dell. There is also a lively description of kissing under the mistletoe* and the customs of snapdragon* and the wassail bowl*.

Plays In addition to the Bethlehem* scenes in mystery plays*, several dramatic productions have been associated with the Christmas season. Amongst the earliest are nativity plays by Lopez de Vega (1612), Ben Jonson's *Christmas His Masque* (1616) and the slight *Mother Shipton's Christmas Carols* (1668). During the eighteenth and nineteenth centuries Christmas plays were mostly in the form of pantomimes*. The ever-popular children's play by J.M. Barrie, *Peter Pan,* was first performed at the Duke of York Theatre on 27 December 1904. More recently there have been A.A. Milne's *Toad of Toad Hall* (with Richard Goolden), stage versions of the television opera *Amahl and the Night Visitors*, and many seasonal plays for theatre, radio and television. (See **Films**)

Plough Sunday The Sunday when the plough is blessed in church at the start of the farming year. Traditionally the first Sunday after Epiphany*, it is followed by Plough Monday when human Plough Stots (bullocks) take the plough round the neighbourhood, performing sword dances in places like Goathland and Knaresborough in Yorkshire. In the old days householders who refused to offer a gift or hospitality sometimes had the land in front of their house ploughed up. (See **Sword Dancing**)

Plum When used in connection with Christmas dishes the term 'plums' sometimes refers to prunes (i.e. dried plums) but more usually to raisins, which were an ingredient of Christmas pies* (e.g. the plum extracted by Jack Horner*), plum puddings* and the game of snapdragon*.

Plum Pudding An old name for Christmas pudding, which was originally plum porridge or plum pottage. (See **Christmas Pudding**)

Plygain From the Welsh for 'cock-crow'*, this is a candlelit carol* service once held in churches and chapels all over Wales around 4 a.m. on Christmas Day* to herald the birth of Christ*. It has medieval origins, and was first observed in Anglican churches, then in Methodist chapels.

Poetry In addition to the verse set to music as carols* and hymns there are some fine poems, ideal for both private and public reading at Christmas. These range from Ben Jonson's 'Hymn on the Nativity of my Saviour' and

Plate 9:
Santa Claus, as conceived by Thomas Nast (1840-1902).
A coloured version of his drawing in *Harper's Weekly* (1881).

Friday *the Four and twentieth day of* December, 1652.

Resolved by the Parliament,

That the Markets be kept to Morrow, being the Five and twentieth day of *December*; And that the Lord Major, and Sheriffs of *London* and *Middlesex*, and the Justices of Peace for the City of *Westminster* and Liberties thereof, do take care, That all such persons as shall open their Shops on that day, be protected from VVrong or Violence, and the Offenders punished.

Resolved by the Parliament,

That no Observation shall be had of the Five and twentieth day of *December*, commonly called *Christmas-Day*; nor any Solemnity used or exercised in Churches upon that Day in respect thereof.

Ordered by the Parliament,

That the Lord Major of the City of *London*, and Sheriffs of *London* and *Middlesex*, and the Justices of Peace of *Middlesex* respectively, be Authorized and Required to see this Order duly observed within the late Lines of Communication, and weekly Bills of Mortality.

Hen: *Scobell*, *Cleric. Parliamenti.*

London, Printed by *John Field*, Printer to the Parliament of *England*. 1652.

Plate 10:
Puritan Act of Parliament abolishing Christmas, 1652
Facsimile reproduction

Plate 11:
Stamp Designs
Christmas Traditions, 1986
The Glastonbury Thorn
The Devil's Knell
The Hereford Boy Bishop
The Tanad Valley Plygain.

Here Mother Shipton, Good Old Dame,
With Harlequin does Kindred Claim.
Perſuades the Father to be Kind;
And Makes each Lover bleſt in Mind,
Turn up and See the happy End,
Which will on Conſtancy Attend.

Plate 12:
Pantomime characters in the 1770s, including Mother Shipton,
Harlequin and Columbine.

Plate 13:

Top – The Twelve Days of Christmas – a compact reminder by W. D. Underwood

Bottom – 'Adeste Fideles' as depicted in an early manuscript

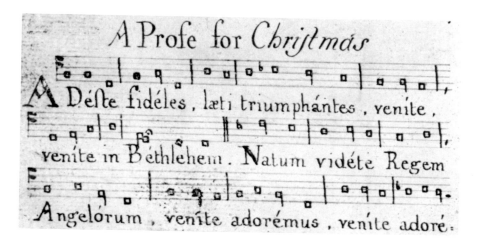

Plate 14:
Presents under a decorated Christmas Tree

Plate 15:
Saint Nicholas, as reconstructed from his skull by Manchester University, 2004.

Plate 16:
A Modern Chinese Nativity, The Magi, by He Qi

Milton's 'Ode on the Morning of Christ's Nativity' to Dylan Thomas's *A Child's Christmas in Wales*, and the ever-popular poem by John Betjeman, with many more available in anthologies, including the *Oxford Book of Christmas Poems* and the author's *Kellett's Christmas*.

Poinsettia This scarlet-topped Mexican plant has recently become established worldwide as a Christmas decoration*. It is named after Dr Joel R. Poinsett of Charlestown, South Carolina, who first introduced it into North America in 1828. A Mexican legend explains its origin in the following incident. The people of Cuernavaca were on their way to Midnight Mass*, all bearing some small gift for the Christ-child. One poor girl, who had nothing to bring, was told by an angel* to pick a wayside plant.

When she did so the topmost leaves burst into flame, and the Poinsettia has done so ever since at Christmas, hence its Mexican name – *Flor de fuego* or 'fire-flower', also called *Flor de Noche Buena* ('Flower of the Holy Night'). Strictly speaking, it is the bright scarlet bracts it is known for, rather than the tiny yellow flowers.

Poland The Polish celebration of Christmas is rich in Catholic traditions, starting with the visit of St Nicholas* on 6 December. Christmas Eve is a time of fasting, broken only when the first star is seen and *oplatek* is eaten. This is a specially baked round wafer, stamped with a nativity scene. The celebratory meal, held before midnight, contains no meat, but usually a fish dish of carp. The climax is when the Star Man enters, accompanied by the Star Boys who sing carols*.

Cribs* are especially important in Poland, and some take the form of little puppet theatres in which the nativity is re-enacted. A Polish carol known all over the world is the fourteenth century '*W zlobie lsezy*', translated as 'Infant holy, Infant lowly'.

Pork Eating pork in all its forms – roast joints, hams, stand pies, sausages, brawn* etc. – is a well-established Christmas tradition from the remotest past. The ceremonial slaughter of a pig was part of the Roman* festival of Saturnalia*, but pork was much more important to the Scandinavians*, who regarded it as the food of the gods in Valhalla. At their festival of Yule-tide* they sacrificed a pig to the goddess Freya – a custom which survived in the medieval feast of the boar's head*. In Victorian times pork was a favourite meat along with goose or turkey, and was also used in stand pies. In *Great Expectations* (1861) Charles Dickens* refers to Pip stealing for the convict 'a beautiful round, compact pork pie'.

At the present time roast pork is second only to turkey* in popularity. It is often served during the Christmas season with the traditional accompaniment of apple sauce and sage-and-onion stuffing.

Port A sweet, fortified wine associated with Christmas, along with sherry*. Its name comes from Oporto, the town in Portugal.

Present-giving The exchange of little gifts during the winter solstice* celebrations dates back at least to the Romans* (See **Saturnalia, Kalends**), and the tradition was reinforced amongst Christians by the Gospel references to the gifts brought by the three Wise Men*.

The emphasis on giving to children*, especially vicariously through some gift-bringer, is several centuries old, as in the visits by St Nicholas*, Baboushka*, Befana*, etc. From the early nineteenth century Santa Claus* has been an essential provider of presents for children, at least in the more affluent parts of the world. It is in these countries that the exchange of Christmas presents amongst adults has become the basis of a vast commercial operation. The earlier simple presents, often personal and home-made, have been replaced by expensive and extravagant items on such a scale that there has been opposition from groups like SCROOGE (Society to Curtail Ridiculous, Outrageous and Ostentatious Gift Exchanges), founded in America in 1979. (See **Christmas Stocking, Toys and Games**)

Prophecy Readings of prophecies from the Old Testament of the coming of the Messiah* or Christ* are commonly heard at Christmas-time, especially in the Festival of Nine Lessons and Carols*. Some of these are quoted in the Gospel accounts of the nativity*. For example, that the child would be born of a virgin, who would call him Immanuel* (Isaiah 7.14), and that this would take place in Bethlehem* (Micah 5.2-5). The idea that the birth was the fulfilment of prophecy provides the opening lines of one of our oldest carols:

> A virgin most pure, as the prophets do tell
> Hath brought forth a baby, as it hath befell ...

Pub Carols Carols* sung in certain pubs in South Yorkshire in places like Stannington and Dungworth, near Sheffield. These include glees, such as 'Hail, Smiling Morn!', carols such as 'Sweet Bells' and others by local composers, some from the late eighteenth century, most of which are which are now unknown to carol singers in general.

Punch A hot drink especially associated with Christmas and New Year*. It is said to have originated in India and to owe its name to the Hindi word *panch*, meaning 'five' – a reference to its five basic ingredients. These are traditionally hot water, wine or spirits, lemons, sugar and spices*.

Puritans The Puritans were remarkable for their attempt to abolish Christmas*, both in England and America in the middle of the seventeenth century. Dislike of a custom which had pagan origins and was popular in 'popish' countries had already appeared in Elizabethan times, and by 1644 Parliament had begun to sit on Christmas Day*, a practice which was to last until 1656. After the execution of Charles I in 1649 Oliver Cromwell strongly attacked the keeping of Christmas. His Parliamentary soldiers confiscated any meat being cooked for Christmas, and suppressed pro-Christmas riots in London and Oxford.

In 1652 Christmas was made illegal by a special Act of Parliament, which declared that shops and markets should be opened and that 'no Observation shall be had of the Five and twentieth day of December, commonly called "Christmas Day" '. The prohibition even extended to singing carols* and going to church. Some Puritans were fanatical in their opposition to observing Christmas Day, Hezekiah Woodward's tract (1652) describing it as 'the old Heathen's Feasting Day ... the Superstitious Man's Idol Day, the Multitude's Idle Day, Satan's Working Day'. Such narrow-minded zealots met with lively opposition in such tracts as *The Vindication of Christmas*, but the diarist John Evelyn records that on Christmas Day 1657 soldiers entered the church where he was about to take communion, pointed their muskets at him, then arrested him for breaking the law. It was said by the poet John Taylor that even eating a mince pie* could lead to arrest on a charge of high treason.

In 1659 the new American colony of Massachusetts Bay fined anyone keeping Christmas five shillings. Even as early as 1620, soon after the Pilgrim Fathers had landed in New England, they had deliberately worked all through Christmas Day to build their log cabins. The law of 1659 was fortunately repealed in 1681, but lingered on in New England, and in some parts Christmas Day did not become a legal holiday until 1856.

After the Restoration of Charles II in 1660, the festival in England soon recovered its traditional vigour, though there was still a rearguard action, indicated by the pamphlet *The Examination and Trial of Old Father Christmas* (1678), and the Puritan attitude to Catholic tradition survives in Scotland, where – ever since the Calvinistic influence of John Knox – it has been customary to celebrate at Hogmanay* and New Year* rather more than at Christmas. (See **Glastonbury Thorn**)

Quaaltagh A Manx name for the first person, male or female, to enter a house on the Isle of Man on New Year's Day. (See **First Footing, New Year**)

Queen Elizabeth II Her Majesty the Queen carries on the royal tradition of spending Christmas at Windsor Castle, and of making the Christmas Day broadcast to the nation and the Commonwealth, the latter begun by her grandfather George V in 1932. She also continues the ancient custom of receiving a spray of Glastonbury Thorn* for her Christmas table and of making the token presentation of gold*, frankincense* and myrrh* at the Chapel Royal at Epiphany. (See **Christmas Day Broadcasts, Epiphany, Glastonbury Thorn**)

Queen of Light A Scandinavian* figure, especially associated with Sweden. She can be traced back to St Lucia*, who defied the Emperor Diocletian by performing works of Christian charity* and who was martyred by him by 303 AD. Although Lucia lived in the Mediterranean area (Syracuse, Sicily), according to an old legend she visited Sweden during a severe famine on the darkest night of the year, bearing lights and a shipload of food. On her feast day (13 December) it is traditional for a girl – often a youngest daughter – to dress up as the Queen of Light (or a 'Lucia Queen' or 'Lucia Bride'), wearing a white dress, with a red sash and a crown of lighted candles*. Accompanied by her attendants she visits her family, friends and neighbours very early in the morning while it is still dark, bringing them coffee and specially baked 'Lucia rolls'. She and her attendants traditionally sing 'Santa Lucia', an old song from Sicily.

Queen's College Queen's College, Oxford, is notable for two ancient traditions: the famous boar's head ceremony which dates back to the fourteenth century, and the custom of the Bursar who presents each college member with a needle threaded with coloured silk on New Year's Day, at the same time saying, 'Take this and be thrifty.' The latter custom is said to date from 1341, when the founder of the college, Robert de Eglesfield, started it because of a French pun on his name (*aiguilles et fil* – needles and thread). (See **Boar's Head, Boar's Head Carol, Pork**)

Quelle est cette odeur agréable? An unusual French carol*, which imagines a visit by the shepherds* to the stable at Bethlehem, to which they are drawn by a delightful fragrance issuing from it.

Quirinius According to St Luke, Quirinius (Cyrenius in Greek) was the Governor of Syria, the Roman province which included Palestine, when Jesus* was born – an additional period of office earlier than that mentioned by Josephus.

Reindeer Reindeer have an ancient association with the midwinter festival of peoples living near the Arctic Circle, who depended on them for food*, clothing and transport, but the association of reindeer with Santa Claus is comparatively recent. The idea seems to have originated in 1821

in an American book for little children, which included colour prints of Santa Claus sitting in a sleigh pulled by a single reindeer. It was then popularized by the publication in 1823 of the poem 'The Night before Christmas' or 'A Visit from St Nicholas' by Clement C. Moore, who not only depicted Santa Claus arriving on 'a miniature sleigh' which was pulled by 'eight tiny reindeer', but gave each of them a name: Dasher, Dancer, Prancer, Vixen, Comet, Cupid, Donder and Blitzen! (See **Santa Claus**)

Although the forerunner of Father Christmas*, Odin*, was said to ride through the sky on a supernatural horse, and was sometimes said to have had a sleigh pulled by goats, the idea of Santa Claus riding on a sleigh pulled by several reindeer has been fixed in the popular imagination ever since the illustrations for Moore's poem. The idea that reindeer could fly through the sky has been linked with the shamans of Lapland* and Siberia, who had delusions of flying induced by hallucinogenic mushrooms.

Reindeer would certainly be suitable for pulling the famous sledge. They are immensely strong and can easily pull twice their own weight. They are very sure-footed on ice because of their concave hoofs, and they are spectacular in appearance, the only deer in which both male and female have antlers.

Réveillon (See **France**)

Richmond Poor Aud 'Oss Central figure in an old Christmas mummers' play at Richmond, North Yorkshire. The horse, played by a dancer in a disguise that includes a real horse's skull, leads a party of red-coated huntsmen round the houses and pubs, where he dies and comes back to life again. (See **Mummers**)

Robin The association of the robin with Christmas can be explained by the fact that this bold and cheery little bird is very conspicuous in midwinter and especially attractive against a background of snow. Because it is preparing to choose a mate at this time of the year, the male robin's song can be heard when most other birds are silent. Male and female robins are so similar in appearance – unlike most birds, where only the male is brightly coloured – which probably gave rise to the old belief that the robin's mate was the wren.

The red breast of the robin has made it the subject of several old legends. It was said that the bird brought fire to the earth, which associated it with the winter solstice*, and it was sacred to the god Thor*. Robins were kept in cages in Roman* courts, and it was said that if a robin sang after a prisoner had been tried he was automatically released.

A robin is said to have been present at the Roman trial of Jesus* before Pontius Pilate. The bird is supposed to have perched on the crown of thorns, and the origin of its red breast is explained by the fact that the bird was smeared with blood when it plucked out a thorn and later tried to comfort Jesus during the crucifixion. The robin is also said to have led Mary Magdalene to the garden tomb of Jesus, and to have sung when Jesus was born – a song which it repeats every Christmas Day*.

The link between the robin and Christmas was strengthened by the introduction of the Penny Post in 1840. The fact that Victorian postmen wore bright red uniforms gave them the nickname of Robin Postmen or Redbreasts. Some of the earliest Christmas cards* depict a robin bringing the Christmas post in its beak, and from 1862 the redbreast has been a standard feature of Christmas cards*. Curiously enough, on Victorian cards there were sometimes pictures of dead robins, probably because of their association with the wren and the ancient custom of hunting these birds. (See also **Round Robin, Wren**)

Romans The Romans made a considerable contribution to our Christmas and New Year* traditions, much of the atmosphere of their convivial public holiday being found in our modern festivities. (See **Saturnalia, Kalends**)

Rosemary A traditional Christmas decoration*, much favoured in earlier times because it is one of the few evergreens which are sweetly scented. It was used by the Romans* during the festival of Saturnalia*, and in medieval England was particularly associated with the boar's head* as is indicated by the lines:

> The boar's head in hand bring I,
> With garland gay and rosemary.

Various superstitions and legends are connected with rosemary. It was said, for example, that Mary*, during the escape to Egypt*, hung the baby's clothes to dry on bushes of rosemary, which is said to bloom only at midnight on Old Christmas Eve, and whose flowers are said to have absorbed the blue tint from Mary's robe. The shrub is supposed to grow erect for 33 years (the lifetime of Jesus) after which it will branch out.

Ripon Cathedral had an ancient custom involving rosemary, which only died out in the middle of the nineteenth century. During the Christmas morning service a procession of choirboys entered the cathedral carrying baskets from which they distributed red apples* and a sprig of rosemary to each member of the congregation.

Round Robin This term was originally used to describe a petition or letter of protest around which the signatures were written in a circular form, so that no individual headed the list. In recent times 'a round robin' is used incorrectly or facetiously to mean a duplicated letter of family news sent out with Christmas cards*, often satirized for its banality, boastfulness and boredom.

Rudolph, the Red-Nosed Reindeer Originally a verse for an advertising campaign, written in 1939 by Robert L. May for a department store in Chicago. Though a trivial tale about a young misfit of a reindeer who helps Santa Claus* by lighting the way with his shiny red nose, it became very popular in the USA*, and is now known especially through the song, written by Johnny Marks in 1947. Two years later the version sung by Gene Autry sold two million copies in the first year.

Rum This spirit, distilled from the residue of sugar cane, is especially popular at Christmas-time, when it is used as a flavouring, mainly in rum sauce or rum butter as an accompaniment to Christmas pudding*.

Russia Christians in post-communist Russia now have full freedom to celebrate Christmas, recovering something of the splendour of the Greek Orthodox ritual which existed before the Revolution of 1917. Many thousands now join the candlelit processions on Christmas Eve known as the *Krestny Khod*, walking round the outside of the church before entering to sing carols and celebrate Midnight Mass*. There is also the traditional twelve-course meatless meal on Christmas Eve. (See **Ukraine**)

Although Grandfather Frost (with the Snow Maiden), artificially introduced by the communist regime to replace the Christian tradition, is still an important gift-bringer, both on Christmas Eve (6 January, following the Julian Calendar) and at New Year*, there are also visits from the patron saint of Russia, St Nicholas, or Santa Claus, and at Epiphany* from *Baboushka** (grandmother), a costumed lady who brings gifts to the children*, similar to her Italian equivalent. (See **Befana**)

St Francis St Francis of Assisi (1181-1226) is associated with Christmas, firstly because he is said to have encouraged the singing of carols*, and secondly because he has been credited with setting up the first nativity scene, or crib*. This took place at Greccio in Northern Italy in 1223, following permission from Pope Honorius III. Although there are earlier references to some form of model depicting the nativity*, especially to the Church of Santa Maria Maggiore in Rome (eighth century), it seems that St Francis and his itinerant friars did much to popularize the use of the *presepio* or nativity scene in churches. The one he made at Greccio included a real ox and ass eating hay. (See **Nativity Scene**)

St Lucia St Lucia (or Lucy) is especially important in Sweden, where her Feast Day (13 December) marks the beginning of the Christmas celebrations. (See **Queen of Light**)

St Nicholas A historical figure who is the basis of the legendary Santa Claus*, a name which is derived from the Dutch version of St Nicholas, *Sinter Klaas*. He was born in the latter part of the third century at Patara in Asia Minor and eventually became the Bishop of Myra, a town further along the Mediterranean coast (now part of south-western Turkey). He had an adventurous life, was imprisoned and tortured by the Roman* Emperor Diocletian, and gained a reputation for courage and generosity, especially towards children*. The two most famous stories concerning him tell of his miraculous restoring to life of three little boys, who had been dismembered and pickled in brine-tubs (as a substitute for pork!) by a wicked innkeeper, and of his secret gift of money (either three golden coins or three small bags of gold*), which saved three girls from being sold into slavery and prostitution. (See **Christmas Stocking**)

Nicholas died around 352 AD, and in 1089 his bones were said to have been stolen and transferred to the Church of San Nicola in the Italian town of Bari, which became a profitable place of pilgrimage, and has recently been made more accessible by the Turkish government. The bones – said to produce a kind of miraculous manna, collected by a priest in a flask each year – were exhumed in 1953 and again in 2004, when the skull was used to make a reconstruction of the face of St Nicholas by Manchester University.

Nicholas became one of the most popular figures in the Greek Orthodox Church: the patron saint of children, sailors, parish clerks and pawnbrokers (whose sign of three golden balls is derived from the three golden coins) and the patron saint of Greece, Russia, and of the city of Aberdeen and other places, with around 400 churches dedicated to St Nicholas in Britain alone.

However, his greatest influence is seen in the tradition of Santa Claus, which preserves the teaching of Jesus* that gifts should be made in secret, without the giver requiring thanks (Matthew 6.1-4). The feast day of St Nicholas is 6 December, on the eve of which he visits schools and homes in Holland* and parts of Germany* and Switzerland. On this occasion he not only carries a sack of presents to reward good children, but is traditionally accompanied by Zwarte Piet*, or some other sinister figure, who is supposed to punish children who have been naughty. (See **Holland, Knecht Ruprecht, Krampus, Père Fouettard**)

St Stephen (See **Feast of Stephen**)

St Thomas Popularly known as 'Doubting Thomas', because he at first would not believe in the resurrection of Jesus*, he is believed to have become the first missionary to India, where he was martyred. His connection with Christmas is that 21 December, the day of the winter solstice*, is also St Thomas's Day. An old country saying ran :

> St Thomas gray, St Thomas gray,
> Longest night and shortest day.

St Thomas's Day, which used to be regarded as the opening day of the Christmas season, was the traditional time to pay out charities* and exercise benevolence. In medieval York, for example, it was proclaimed that thieves and prostitutes would be welcome to the city, to join in the boisterous festivities being led by the characters 'Yule' and 'Yule's Wife'. In some parts of England the poor went 'Thomasing', begging for gifts of money or provisions, such as flour to make the Christmas bread. On St Thomas' Eve it was once the custom for unmarried girls to stick nine pins into a peeled onion, saying:

> Good St Thomas, do me right,
> Send me my true love this night.

Other St Thomas' Day traditions were candle auctions and the custom of children having the right to prevent the master entering the school until granted a holiday. (See **Barring-out, Candle Auctions**)

Santa Claus The mysterious, supernatural figure who brings presents to children during the night of Christmas Eve, so that they wake up on Christmas morning to find them at the foot of the bed, traditionally in a stocking, more recently in a pillowcase, which they have left there the previous night in confident expectation of it being filled with good things. In France*, for example, it is the tradition to put out shoes – a variation of the legend about the anonymous gifts of St Nicholas, which could have fallen into shoes round the fireplace as easily as into stockings hanging up to dry.

The name Santa Claus is derived from *Sinter Klaas,* the Dutch pronunciation of St Nicholas. In the late seventeenth century the name and traditions surrounding Nicholas were introduced into America by Dutch Protestant settlers. It is said that the first of their ships to reach Manhattan Island had St Nicholas as its figurehead. The Dutch settled mainly in New Amsterdam, later known as New York, and from here the Santa Claus legend eventually spread throughout North America, and then to England, where it merged during the second half of the nineteenth century with a parallel tradition of even greater antiquity, that of Father Christmas.

In 1809 Washington Irving* wrote about the legendary Santa Claus riding through the sky with a horse pulling a wagon-load of presents, which he dropped down the chimneys, filling stockings hanging by the fireplace. The wagon was pulled by a horse, but in 1821 the American publication *The Children's Friend* included coloured pictures showing, for the first time, Santa Claus on a sleigh pulled by a reindeer, flying

> O'er chimney tops and tracks of snow
> To bring his yearly gifts to you.

Two years later this image of Santa Claus was further developed and popularized by a 56-line poem, 'A Visit from Saint Nicholas', which appeared anonymously on 23 December 1823 in a New York paper called the *Troy Sentinel.* Its much-quoted opening lines were:

> 'Twas the night before Christmas and all through the house
> Not a creature was stirring, not even a mouse ...

The poem was later discovered to have been written by Dr Clement C. Moore, a professor of Hebrew at Columbia University. He had composed it simply to amuse his own children the previous Christmas Eve, and is said to have got the idea after a sleigh-ride delivering Christmas presents, and to have based Santa Claus on a genial old Dutchman who did odd jobs for him. Another story is that he based it on an earlier poem written by Henry Livingston.

Though Moore did not invent Santa Claus, he helped to form the popular image, depicting him as jolly, chubby and red-nosed, with a white beard, though he was dressed in fur, dirtied with soot, and he smoked a pipe. He looked like a kind of elf (small enough to get down chimneys), and had a sleigh pulled by eight tiny reindeer for whom Moore invented names. (For these and a comment on flying, see **Reindeer**.)

Moore's children, and others, would surely not have been frightened by this friendly, good-humoured visitor:

> He had a broad face and a little round belly
> That shook when he laughed, like bowl-ful of jelly.

A reminder of the original priestly garments of St Nicholas seems to survive in the red robe, with a hood fringed with fur, and in Holland*, and parts of Germany* and Switzerland, the figure portraying St Nicholas wears a bishop's mitre and carries a crook. Whereas T.C. Boyd, Moore's illustrator in 1848, showed St Nicholas wearing a fur cap and a short coat with buckled shoes, the fur-trimmed robe worn by a normal-sized man was depicted by Thomas Nast in his popular drawings of Santa Claus. These appeared in the Christmas number of the American *Harper's Weekly* from 1863 – the first showing him visiting a civil war camp of soldiers, since Nast was a supporter of Abraham Lincoln and the North. His Santa, however, wears a fur-edged cap rather than a hood, and smokes a long-stemmed clay pipe. He is also very corpulent and wears a broad belt with a prominent buckle.

Pictures in magazines and on Christmas cards*, showing him in his scarlet robe (sometimes it had been green or white) and black boots had quickly established the accepted Santa Claus outfit by the end of the nineteenth century. This was partly through the influence of illustrations by the German artist, Moritz Von Schwind (1804-71), but the most influential of all the pictures of Santa Claus were those in the Coca-Cola adverts. The first, by the Swedish artist Haddon Sundblom appeared in 1931 and showed a cheery, white-haired old gentleman, beaming with benevolence.

German settlers in the state of Indiana founded a town on Christmas Eve 1852 and called it Santa Claus. In 1935 a huge statue of Santa was erected in the park there and dedicated 'to the children of the world in memory of an undying love'. The town runs special training courses for prospective Santas who intend to work in stores and at parties, and who receive the diploma of 'Bachelor of Santa Claus'. There is now a vast money-spinning Santa Claus industry, with its training centres, annual conference and Santa Claus diplomas. At Newton in Powys, Wales, there is an annual Santa Run in which thousands of costumed Santas run 4.5 miles for charity.*

Children find it difficult to reconcile the bogus and sometimes casual, half-disguised Santa Clauses of stores and parties with the excitingly supernatural figure who visits them on Christmas Eve. In spite of Santa Claus being grossly commercialized and treated as a joke he still manages to provide annual delight for untold millions of young children, whose parents have the imagination to sustain the folklore which surrounds him.

A well-established tradition is to write notes to Santa Claus (alias Father Christmas), requesting presents. This may be either through the post or by e-mail, usually addressed to the North Pole (Greenland) or Lapland* (Northern Finland*), where he has rival official residences, or by sending them up the chimney (by convection current!). The idea that Santa Claus came down the chimney – feasible in the days of wide fireplaces – may have originated in the ancient belief that witches could enter houses like this, or possibly from the Siberian custom of entering primitive homes through the smoke-hole. Dutch children sometimes leave carrots in their shoes for the horse of St Nicholas, and many young English children leave some refreshment for Santa Claus in the fireplace: a mince pie* and a glass of milk, for example, with a carrot for the reindeer. (See also **Father Christmas, St Nicholas, Christmas Stocking**)

Santons Small French figures for the nativity scene* carved from wood or sculpted in clay. Originally coming to Provence from Italy*, they are now especially associated with Aubagne, near Marseilles, where there is an annual *Santons* fair.

Saturnalia The Roman* festival held around the time of the winter solstice*. Originally it must have been one of the prehistoric ceremonies to revive the dying sun, but to the Romans it was essentially a celebration of the return of the sun, and the high point of the festival was called *Dies Natalis Solis Invicti* – the Birthday of the Unconquered Sun. This was held on 25 December, a day sacred to Mithras, a sun-god of Persian origin, and to Attis, a Phrygian god – both of whom, incidentally, required their devotees to be baptized in the blood of a slaughtered bull. The connection with Saturn is obscure, but it may be explained by the myth that Saturnus, an agricultural god, had been welcomed to Rome with great feasting by Janus, the two-headed god whose name we still use our word January.

Saturnalia lasted more than a week, usually from 17-28 December, and was a time of riotous merrymaking, with fires and illuminations. Homes, streets and temples were decorated with evergreens*, and presents were exchanged, including little dolls of terracotta (*signilloria*) and wax tapers (*cerei*). In Rome a pig was sacrificed in the temple of Saturn in the Forum, and this was followed by great feasts, which often led to drunkenness and debauchery. It was a Saturnalian tradition that society should be made topsy-turvy. The men dressed up as women, and the women as men. (See **Pantomime**) The slaves were dressed up, given a temporary badge of freedom (*pilleus*) and sat at lavishly-spread tables, where they were waited upon by their lords and masters, a custom which survives today in the armed services, when officers serve the Christmas dinner to their men. In Roman times some sort of control over the general anarchy was exercised by a mock king, the ancestor of the Lord of Misrule*.

Along with the northern Yule-tide* the festival of Saturnalia is an obvious forerunner of the modern Christmas. (For an explanation of the connection see **Christmas, Christmas Day, Kalends**)

Scandinavians In the ninth century the Vikings, from Norway, Denmark and Sweden, helped to establish in England the ancient festival of Yule-tide*, which took place in honour of their gods such as Odin* and goddesses such as Freya at the time of the winter solstice*. The festival was already known to the Anglo-Saxons* who, when they became Christians, eventually replaced Yule-tide with Christmas, especially under the influence of Alfred the Great, who succeeded in halting the Scandinavian invasion.

Many of the Christmas traditions in modern Scandinavia are of great antiquity and interest. In Norway there is the brewing of *juleol*, a special beer for Christmas, the eating of *lutefisk*, a cod dish, and the sheaf of oats or wheat called the *julenek*, set up on a pole as a Christmas treat for the birds. In Sweden there is the lovely female herald of Christmas, St Lucy (see **Queen of Light**), an especially lavish Christmas *smorgasbord*, and a final fling on 13 January, when Christmas is officially driven out by St Knut (King Canute). In Denmark there is a special meal on Christmas Eve, usually featuring roast goose*, and a kind of rice porridge in which a lucky almond is hidden. Amongst seasonal confectionary is *speculatius*, a rich biscuit made by pressing the dough into moulds of Christmas shapes. In common with Britain the Danes listen to a royal broadcast, but on New Year's Eve. Danish traditions are also found in Iceland, which has several of its own, including the *Jolasveinar*, the thirteen mysterious Yule Goblins. (For other Scandinavian traditions see **Boar's Head, Hodening, Julebuck, Julklapp, Pork and Up-Helly-Aa**)

Scrooge The immortal character Ebenezer Scrooge appears in the story by Charles Dickens*, *A Christmas Carol**, published in December 1843. He is said to be based on a notorious skinflint of the previous century, Daniel Dancer of Harrow. He also seems to be a development of the mean-spirited, Christmas-hating grave-digger, Gabriel Grub, featured by Dickens in *Pickwick Papers** (1837). The miserly Scrooge, whose attitude to Christmas is summed up by the phrase 'Bah! Humbug!', is completely reformed after he is visited by the ghosts* of Christmas Past, Present and Future, and finally shows great kindness to the impoverished Bob Cratchit and his family, especially to Tiny

138

Tim*. A 'Scrooge' has become a synonym for somebody who disapproves of the celebration of Christmas, and it is arguable that because of the enduring power of the image created by Dickens comparatively few – people like George Bernard Shaw, for example – have dared to be so contemptuous of the festive season, least of all to attempt to ban it like the Puritans*. (See **Abolition of Christmas**)

Shepherds Though romantically portrayed in nativity plays* and many pictures of Christmas, shepherds in first-century Palestine were regarded by their fellow-Jews as ceremonially unclean and amongst the lowest in society. The carol* is right to describe them as 'certain poor shepherds', and it is significant that the announcement of the birth of Jesus* was first given to them and not to the high and mighty, and that it was they who had the first privileged peep at the new-born baby (Luke 2.9-20).

Shepherds' Field An attractive rural site just south-east of Bethlehem*, shown to pilgrims and tourists as the place where the 'shepherds* watched their flocks by night'. A neat modern chapel has been built here near the ruins of a fifth-century church and an ancient cave.

Sherry Like port* this is a fortified wine associated with Christmas, originally from Spain* and named after the town in Andalucia, Jerez de la Frontera.

Silent Night One of the most popular of Christmas carols*, translated from the Austrian* verses beginning *Stille Nacht, heilige Nacht,* written by Joseph Mohr (1792-1848). There are several English versions, few of which are really close to the original German*, and which usually include only the first two and last verses from the original six.

'Silent night' has a particularly interesting history. It originated just before Christmas 1818, when Joseph Mohr, assistant priest of St Nicholas's Church in the riverside village of Oberndorf, near Salzburg, discovered that the church organ was useless because mice had eaten a hole in the bellows. So he decided to improvise a Christmas hymn suitable for less formal singing, using the words of a poem he had written two years earlier. He then invited his friend, Franz Gruber (1787-1863), a village schoolmaster, who was also the church organist, to set his words to music. This Franz did just in time for the Christmas service, playing the accompaniment on his guitar, and singing it as a duet with Joseph.

The carol was an immediate success, and spread from the village to other parts of Austria, mainly through the enthusiasm of a man who came to repair the organ, Karl Mauracher. He was so impressed when he heard Gruber play it on the newly-repaired organ that he took the carol with him, and later taught it to the four children* of the Strasser family. It became known as 'The Song from Heaven', and the Strasser children became so famous for their singing of it that on Christmas Eve 1832 they were invited to sing it before the King and Queen in the Royal Saxony Court Chapel, from where it spread throughout the world, translated into around 200 languages. (See **Stamps**)

Snapdragon A lively, traditional Christmas game which, like the custom of lighting brandy* on a Christmas pudding*, probably has its roots in the prehistoric ritual of lighting fires to revive the dying sun at the winter solstice*. It consists of placing in a shallow dish raisins which have been soaked in brandy, and which are now set alight. The game – played in the dark – is to snatch a raisin (or 'plum') without being burnt by the weirdly snapping blue flames of the 'dragon'. A traditional song or rhyme accompanying the game included the lines:

> With his blue and lapping tongue
> Many of you will be stung;
> Snip! Snap! Dragon!
> For he snaps at all that comes,
> Snatching at his feast of plums ...

Snapdragon was a standard game for Christmas Eve as recently as Victorian times. Charles Dickens* refers to it in his account of the Christmas at Dingley Dell in his *Pickwick Papers** (1837). 'There was a great game of snapdragon,' he tells us, 'when fingers enough were burned.' (See also **Flapdragon**)

Snow (See **White Christmas**)

Snowman The cartoon story *The Snowman*, by Raymond Briggs, is especially associated with Christmas. First shown on television in 1982, it is remembered especially by the haunting song made popular by Aled Jones.

Song of the Shirt A protest poem by Thomas Hood, outraged by the wretched plight of women workers in sweated-labour shops, published in the Christmas number of *Punch* in 1843, the year of the first Christmas card* and *A Christmas Carol**.

Songs Christmas songs, as distinct from carols*, can contribute greatly to the festive atmosphere. The oldest, which has hidden Christian symbolism, is 'The Twelve Days of Christmas'*. More recent are popular songs such as

'Jingle Bells' (1857)*, 'I'm dreaming of a White Christmas' (1942), 'Here comes Santa Claus!' (1946), 'Rudolf the Red-nosed Reindeer' (1947)*, 'Mary's Boy Child' (1956)*, 'Winter Wonderland' (1959), 'Santa Claus is coming to Town' (1960), 'Let it Snow!' (1960), 'Merry Christmas, Everybody!' (1973), 'I wish it could be Christmas every day' (1973), 'Do they know it's Christmas?' (1984) (see **Charities**), 'Mistletoe and Wine' (1988) – and there are continued attempts by singers and pop groups to achieve a 'Christmas Number One'.

Spain Catholic tradition ensures a colourful celebration of Christmas in Spain, beginning on 8 December with *Los Sieses,* in which boys in Seville Cathedral dance to herald in the nativity*, and images of the Virgin are carried through the streets. In addition to the *belen,* or nativity scenes*, and other Christian symbols, there are the more worldly activities of Christmas markets and the *Loteria de Navidad*, said to be the biggest Christmas lottery in the world. Christmas Eve, or *Noche Buena,* is celebrated with Midnight Mass* and a special meal often including turkey*, but also fish dishes. A well-known Spanish sweetmeat is *turrón*, nougat made from almonds. The climax of the season is the *Dia de Reyes* (see **Epiphany**), when there are lively parades and parties centred round the Three Kings, who place presents in shoes left out by the children. A link with customs elsewhere is the eating of the *Rosca de Reyes,* a ring-shaped cake containing either a bean or a porcelain baby doll, as in the *Fête des Rois*. (See **France**).

South America Here Christmas strongly reflects Catholic traditions introduced by the Spanish and Portuguese. In Brazil, for example, children leave out their shoes to be filled with presents by *Papai Noel*, and again at the *Folia de Reis* (Epiphany). Though Latin America in general celebrates Christmas in tropical heat, there is great feasting on turkey*, pork*, fish dishes and local specialities of confectionery.

Spices Indispensable ingredients in many Christmas dishes and drinks, spices have for centuries been prized for their exotic flavour and aroma, linked in the popular imagination with the oriental setting of the nativity*. Originally from the tropical East Indies, spices such as ginger were imported as early as the eleventh century, followed by others brought back during the Crusades. Commonly used at Christmas, in addition to ginger (a root), are cloves (dried flower buds), nutmeg (a large seed), mace (from the covering of nutmegs), allspice (pimento berry) and cinnamon (a tree bark).

Stamps Special Christmas issues of postage stamps started in Canada with a stamp showing a map of the world (with the British Empire in red), and printed over it 'Xmas 1898'. Stamps from Czechoslovakia depicted 'Good King Wenceslas*' from 1929, Christmas symbolism appeared on

Austrian stamps in 1937, and the first set of religious Christmas pictures, showing the shepherds*, angels* and Wise Men* appeared on Hungarian stamps in 1943. An Austrian* stamp depicted the author and composer of 'Silent Night'* on the 130th anniversary of its composition in 1948, and again on the 150th anniversary in 1968. Cuba began issuing Christmas stamps in 1951, at first religious, recently more secular. Australia has an impressive set of Christmas issues dating back to 1957, and New Zealand has issued famous Christmas paintings each year since 1960, including some showing the Southern Cross. Canada has kept up the tradition it started, issuing high-quality stamps, mostly with a Christian theme, such as Dürer's *Praying Hands* with the English/French caption *'Christmas-Noël'* in 1966. As this was World Refugee Year the stamps issued in Ireland showed the flight into Egypt*.

There are now at least 50 countries which issue Christmas stamps. A favourite theme is the Madonna* and Child, and every year since 1959 the Vatican has issued a nativity scene* painted by artists of many nationalities. Amongst special British Christmas stamps outstanding themes have been 'The Twelve Days of Christmas'* (1977), Carol Singers (1978), Traditions (1986) and Santa Claus* (2004).

Star of Bethlehem A star of silver or gold, commonly seen in decorations* or on Christmas cards* etc., representing the star which, according to St Matthew's Gospel, was first seen by Magi or Wise Men* in an eastern country, either Persia or Babylon. They interpreted it as announcing the birth of the King of the Jews, set off on the long journey to Jerusalem, and, after Herod's* scribes had told them of the prophecy that the Messiah* would be born in Bethlehem,* they went there, with the star leading them to the actual birthplace (Matthew 2.1-12). Contrary to popular belief, we are not told that the star was seen by the shepherds* and there is no mention at all of a star in St Luke's account of the nativity*, though in describing the angelic visitation to the shepherds he adds: 'And the glory of the Lord shone round around them' (Luke 2.9).

Some critics have dismissed Matthew's account of the star as romantic fabrication, but others have taken the view that it is based on a remarkable astronomical phenomenon which took place when, or shortly before, Jesus* was born (i.e. around 6 BC). One such possible phenomenon is a rare conjunction, which occurs when two or three planets, usually well separated in the sky, are in such a position that from earth they appear to be close together, forming an unusually bright source of light. Johann Kepler (1571-1630), who discovered the laws of planetary motion, was the first to work out that there had been three conjunctions of Jupiter and Saturn in the September of 7 BC in the constellation of Pisces, and this had, in fact, been recorded in cuneiform tablets found in Sippar, near Babylon. The eastern astrologers would not at first have associated the conjunction with the Jewish people, whose sign was Ares, the Ram. However, in 6 BC there was an eclipse of the moon by Jupiter in Ares.

Other theories are that the star was a supernova, an abnormally bright celestial object which suddenly appears when one of the larger stars explodes, radiating energy perhaps 200 million times greater than that of our sun. Supernovae are not common, but can be seen with the naked eye; one lasting 70 days was apparently recorded by the Chinese in 5 BC. A third theory is that it was a comet, a fourth that it was a particularly bright meteor or shooting star. (See **Christmas, Magi**)

Stir-up Sunday The traditional day for making Christmas pudding* – the Sunday before St Andrew's Day (30th November), when the Church of England Collect began: 'Stir up, we beseech thee, O Lord, the wills of thy faithful people'. The phrase 'stir up' was humorously linked with the custom of making sure that each member of the family, with their eyes closed, made a wish, while stirring the pudding mixture from east to west, the direction taken by the Wise Men*. Sometimes children* went through the streets inviting help and singing:

> Stir up, we beseech thee
> The pudding in the pot,
> And when we get home
> We'll eat the lot.

Sussex Carol So called because it was a traditional carol* collected in Sussex by R. Vaughan Williams (1872-1958). It begins: 'On Christmas night all Christians sing'.

Swaddling Clothes The term used in the Authorized Version of the Bible (1611) to translate St Luke's word for the clothing in which Mary* wrapped her new-born baby. As the familiar seventeenth-century carol* rightly says, they were 'swaddling bands' – strips of cloth rather like bandages, in which it was the custom to wrap up very young babies.

143

Sword Dancing A little-known English tradition is the performance of celebratory sword dances during the Christmas season. The climax of each dance is the skilful weaving of the long-swords into a star-shaped 'lock', which

is then held aloft by the squire or leader – a custom thought to be symbolic of the revival of the sun after the winter solstice*. Though mostly extinct, the tradition is observed on Boxing Day* in Yorkshire, both on the coast at Flamborough and in the Sheffield area. (See **Plough Sunday**)

Teddy Bears These first appeared in America at Christmas 1902, following a report that in November the President Theodore ('Teddy') Roosevelt, hunting in the southern states, had refused to shoot a female bear. A cartoon of this in the *New York Times* had the caption 'Teddy's Bear', and this led to the production of the well-known cuddly toy.

Thomasing (See **St Thomas**)

Tinsel Strands of glittering material, usually silver, though occasionally golden or variously coloured. The word has nothing to do with tin, and is derived from the Old French word *estincelle*, meaning 'spark'. The commonest use of tinsel is for the decoration* of Christmas trees* where it gives the impression of sparkling frost or snow on the branches. A legend says that the first tinsel appeared when a poor woman's Christmas tree was visited during Christmas Eve by spiders who covered it with their webs. As a reward for the woman's great virtue the Christ-child is said to have transformed the spiders' webs into strands of silver. Believed to have first been made in Germany* in 1610, originally out of silver beaten wafer-thin, it is now made from foil of other metallic compounds.

Tiny Tim The little crippled boy, Tim Cratchit, in *A Christmas Carol** (1843) by Charles Dickens*. His impending death is shown by the ghost* of Christmas Future to the horrified Scrooge*, who becomes a reformed character, helping the struggling Cratchit family and becoming 'a second father' to Tiny Tim. Dickens has been accused of sentimentality in his portrayal of the character, who is introduced by the words 'Alas, for Tiny Tim, he bore a little crutch, and had his limbs supported by an iron frame!' But there is no denying the powerful impact of Tiny Tim, whose much-quoted Christmas toast closes the story: 'God bless Us, Every One.'

Toys and Games Christmas is toy time, with vast, incalculable amounts spent on children* in the affluent parts of the world, most of the toys now manufactured cheaply in Asian countries. Even in earlier, less prosperous times, children received Christmas presents of toys and games, though most were simple and many were home-made, and there was a limited range, typified by dolls and dolls' houses for girls and toy soldiers, drums and bugles etc. for boys.

In chronological order, here are a few of the of the more recent toys and games marketed at Christmas, starting with modest but well-loved items: Tiddley Winks (1889), Snakes and Ladders (1892), Ludo (1896), Electric trains (1897),

147

Bagatelle (1898), Ping Pong (1900), Meccano (1901), Plasticine (1908), cap guns, water pistols etc. (1920s), Yo-yo (1928), Dinkie Toys (1931), Monopoly (1935), Scrabble, Cluedo (1948), Lego (1955), Corgi Cars (1956), Hula Hoop (1958), Barbie Dolls (1959), Cabbage Patch Dolls (1983), Tamagotchi (1996).

This list goes on and on, many of these introductions being short-lived novelties and mostly discarded, yet some will become valuable collectors' items, especially the wind-up clockwork toys which preceded battery models. In the twenty-first century toys and games may well be sophisticated electronic marvels, yet it is still true that simple things can give the greatest pleasure.

Trifle Made in some form since Tudor times, this is a popular cold dessert, commonly served at Christmas, consisting of a base of sponge, often soaked in sherry*, with layers of fruit* and custard, topped with whipped cream.

Turkey Although not a customary food* for as long as pork* or goose*, for example, roast turkey has been a Christmas dish in England since Tudor times, when it was eaten by Henry VIII, and took its place alongside capon, peacock and swan. By the late 1500s turkey seems to have become more generally accepted, with James I enjoying it at Christmas 1603, and the choice of turkey by the Americans for their first Thanksgiving Day (1621) helped to establish it further. In the following century Benjamin Franklin tried to have the turkey accepted as the national bird of America. By the time of Charles Dickens* it was becoming a popular dish in England, as we are reminded by the fact that the reformed Scrooge* sent a 'prize Turkey' to the Cratchits. It is now standard Christmas fare in many countries, especially Britain, which consumes at least 10 million turkeys each Christmas.

The turkey, native to North and Central America, acquired its name through some misunderstanding, and has nothing whatever to do with the country of the same name, only in so far as it was at first confused with the guinea fowl, which used to be imported via Turkey. The French version was that it came from India – hence their word for turkey, *la dinde* (from *d'Inde*). The first turkeys are believed to have been introduced into Europe from Mexico by the Spanish conquistadores as early as 1519, and were first brought

to England by William Strickland, a Yorkshireman who sailed to America with Sebastian Cabot, and who in 1545 brought back several cages of turkeys which he later bred on the family estate at Boynton, near Bridlington on the Yorkshire coast. In 1550 Strickland was awarded a coat-of-arms by Edward VI which included 'a Turkey in its pride proper'. The lectern in Boynton Church supports the Bible, not by the customary outspread wings of an eagle, but by those of a turkey. William Strickland sent turkeys to Queen Elizabeth I, and the bird was a Christmas favourite not only with James I, but later with George II who kept a flock of 3,000 in Richmond Park.

Norfolk became the principal area for the breeding of turkeys, and by the end of the eighteenth century was sending to London as many as 1,000 turkeys a day, specially shod for the long walk. In the wild, turkeys can grow to a weight of around 17 pounds, but they have been bred to make even bigger birds, to provide the maximum meat. Even in Dickens's day Scrooge bought a turkey so overweight that if it had tried to stand it 'would have snapped its legs off short, like a stick of sealing wax.' For each pound of its weight a turkey should be roasted for approximately 20 minutes. It is traditionally served with stuffing (sausage-meat, chestnut*, sage and onion), bread sauce, cranberry sauce and chipolata sausages, as well as roast potatoes, carrots and Brussels sprouts*. (See **Cranberries**, **Wishbone**)

Turkish Delight   Along with other oriental delicacies, Turkish Delight or *loqum* has a traditional association with Christmas. In Turkey it is usually made from cornstarch, delicately flavoured with lemon, rose perfume etc. and chopped up into pieces which are prevented from sticking by a coating of finely powdered sugar.

Twelfth Cake   (See below, and also **Christmas Cake**)

Twelfth Night   Next to Christmas Day* itself this was once the most popular time for festivities. Twelfth Night falls on 5 January, the eve of Epiphany, which after 1752 was sometimes known as Old Christmas Day*. In earlier times it was celebrated as the evening of Epiphany itself.

From the Middle Ages until early Victorian times Twelfth Night was regarded as the climax of the Christmas season, providing the opportunity for a last fling of dressing-up, merry-making and feasting, with something of the light-hearted atmosphere of Shakespeare's comedy *Twelfth Night*, so called because it was performed on that night in 1601 before Queen Elizabeth I.

Twelfth Night was especially a time for party games*, and in the eighteenth and early nineteenth centuries it was presided over by a king and queen, originally to commemorate the Three Kings or Wise Men*. The royal pair were chosen during the eating of a cake in which was hidden a bean and a pea. The man who found the bean in his portion was king. The woman who found the pea was the queen, or she was chosen by the king or a man who found the pea. Although the custom has now died out in England, it survives in the Baddeley Cake, and is still kept up in France as the *Fête des Rois** and in Spanish-speaking countries as the *Dia de Reyes**.

Twelfth Night was a favourite time for Apple Wassailing* – drinking health amongst rural communities – and in ceremonies connected with blessing the next year's harvest, often round bonfires. In some country districts it was by the lighting of twelve bonfires, representing Jesus* and eleven of the disciples. Sometimes thirteen were lit, but as the thirteenth represented Judas the fire was almost immediately stamped out. (See **Baddeley Cake, Epiphany, France, Spain**)

Twelve Days of Christmas   The official length of the feast of Christmas, proclaimed at the Council of Tours in 567, and later in England by Alfred the Great. Although the phrase is now familiar mainly through the old song bearing this title, it was once customary to keep Christmas from 25 December to 6 January (Epiphany*) so that the Twelve Days are those which come immediately after Christmas Day*, with Twelfth Night* as the climax of the festivities. The reason for this long period is probably twofold. Firstly, the Roman* midwinter festivals of Saturnalia* and Kalends* covered a similar period, and secondly, 6 January would have been Christmas Day if the Julian calendar had not been replaced by the Gregorian. For many years after 1752, when the change took place, it was referred to as 'Christmas Day, Old Style'. (See **Old Christmas Day**). It used to be the custom to eat a mince pie* on each of the Twelve Days of Christmas to ensure 12 'happy months' in the coming year.

Traditionally decorations* are kept up throughout the Twelve Days (including Epiphany) and removed immediately afterwards to avert bad luck. The official church season of Christmas, incidentally, lasts until Candlemas* (2 February), and it used to be the custom to keep up all the Christmas greenery until the Eve of Candlemas.

Twelve Days of Christmas (Song)   The old song beginning 'On the first day of Christmas' is of unknown date and origin, but its curious symbolism may have been to help persecuted Catholics in the late sixteenth century to remember the tenets of their faith. Suggested interpretations include: 1. Partridge in a pear tree (Jesus*), 2. Turtle doves (The Old and New Testaments), 3. French hens (faith, hope and charity*), 4. Calling birds (The Four Gospels), 5. Gold* rings (the first five books of the Old Testament), 6. Geese* (The six days of creation), 7. Swans (the seven sacraments), 8. Maids (the Beatitudes), 9. Ladies (the fruits of the Spirit), 10. Lords (the Ten Commandments), 11. Pipers (the Apostles, without Judas), 12. Drummers (the items of the Apostles' Creed).

Ukraine The Ukraine has a distinctive type of Christmas. Christmas Eve falls on 6 January, and is a solemn memorial of the hardships endured by Mary*. The family gather round a table which is strewn with hay and then covered with a fine, embroidered cloth. A sight of the first star to appear in the eastern sky is a signal for the start of the Holy Supper, which consists of 12 dishes, symbolic of the Apostles. The first of these is *kutya*, consisting of wheat, honey, sugar, nuts and ground poppy seeds. The head of the household greets the family saying '*Kristos Naradywsia!*' ('Christ* is born!') then throws a spoonful of the *kutya* at the ceiling. If it sticks there it is a sign that the family will stay together during the next year. If a member of the family has died during the year an extra place is laid, as Ukrainian Christians believe that souls are reunited on Holy Night. A lighted candle is placed in the window to guide any other souls or strangers who may care to join in the festivities, which are continued through to Christmas Day*, 7 January.

Now that the restraints of communism are removed there is enthusiastic celebration of Christmas by Ukrainians, both in church and through parties of carol* singers going from house to house.

United States of America From 1607 the earliest settlers in Virginia kept a lively English Christmas, with feasting and merriment, but from 1620 the Pilgrim Fathers in New England worked through Christmas, building their homes. These stricter Puritans* objected to the festival to such an extent that in 1659 William Bradford recorded that Massachusetts Bay Colony imposed a fine of five shillings on any colonist who openly kept Christmas, and banned all Christmas music, games* and the eating of mince pies*.

Since then, by contrast, the USA has developed into a country which celebrates Christmas in a lavish and sometimes spectacular way, much influenced by early writers like Washington Irving* and Clement C. Moore, with their promotion of Santa Claus* and present-giving. The spirit of the Victorian English Christmas was further spread through the great popularity of Charles Dickens*, who visited America in 1842 and again in 1868.

The steady evolution of Christmas was interrupted by the catastrophic American Civil War (1861-65), but afterwards the keeping of Christmas was stronger than ever as a time for family reunions and peaceful benevolence. As industry further developed, mass production made the exchange of presents increasingly easy. The commercial aspect of the American Christmas is typified in the opening of the season by the famous Thanksgiving Parade organized in New York by Macy's department store.

Though grossly commercialized, Christmas in the USA has a very high Christian content, seen in crowded church services and carol* concerts, and in customs introduced by immigrants from Holland*, Germany*, Scandinavia*, Italy* and Spanish-speaking countries. This means that there are various festive foods* introduced from abroad, including, for example, the Candy Cane*, a sweetmeat brought by Germans from Cologne, consisting of a stick of red-striped mint rock in the shape of a shepherd's* crook, used to decorate* Christmas trees*.

A number of popular Hollywood films have both illustrated the average American Christmas and influenced the whole world, notably *Holiday Inn* (1942) which contains Bing Crosby's rendition of the phenomenally popular 'I'm dreaming of a White Christmas'. (See **Films, White Christmas**)

Up Helly-Aa The midwinter fire-festival held at Lerwick in the Shetland Islands on the last Tuesday in January, originally the official ending of the old Scandinavian festival of Yule-tide. The ceremony starts at 7.30 p.m. and is led by the Guiser* Jarl, representing an old Norse chieftain. Dressed in armour and wearing a cloak, he stands at the helm of a specially built Viking longboat which is more than nine metres long. This is carried through the streets by guisers singing and brandishing torches, followed by a procession and accompanied by bands. When they reach the official burning-site the marchers form a great circle round the longboat, their torches still blazing. Jarl leaves the ship, and at the sound of a bugle all the torches are thrown into the wooden vessel, which bursts into spectacular flames. Drinking and general revelry continue almost throughout the night. (See **Scandinavians, Yule-tide**)

Venison In Anglo-Saxon* and Norman times there were many wild deer in Britain, but by the early Middle Ages they were being carefully bred and controlled in deer parks and royal forests William the Conqueror was the first to introduce the severe penalty of blinding for the unauthorized killing of deer, and the Robin Hood legends tell of outlaws poaching the royal game. Later, venison was occasionally accessible to ordinary people, and at Christmas was usually served with frumenty*. An early reference to venison for the Christmas table is preserved in the line 'And the running of the deer' in 'The holly and the ivy'*.

Victoria Queen Victoria (1819-1901) did much to encourage the keeping of Christmas as a happy family occasion, and at the same time a religious festival carrying an obligation to show charity* to the poor and needy. There is no doubt that this was influenced through the royal example of Christmases spent at Windsor, fully reported in the *Illustrated London News*, which in 1848 showed the Queen and her family assembled round the Christmas tree* first set up by her German* husband Prince Albert* in 1841.

Victoria's reign also saw the introduction of the first real Christmas card* in 1843, the influential writings of the Christmas enthusiast, Charles Dickens*, the revival of carol* singing, the invention of Christmas crackers and the spread of the Santa Claus* tradition.

Vienna   Vienna is famous for its televised New Year Concerts, typically beginning with an overture by Franz von Suppé, and consisting mainly of waltzes, polkas, marches etc. by the Strauss family.

Virgin Birth   The statement that Jesus* was born of a virgin is made by St Matthew (1.18-25), who emphasizes the embarrassment of Joseph* when he learns that Mary is pregnant, and also by St Luke (1.26-56), who describes Mary's difficulty in accepting the news that she is to conceive a child through the supernatural visitation of the Holy Spirit. The Virgin Birth is also implied in the prologue of St John's Gospel, which declares that 'the Word was made flesh and dwelt among us' (John 1.14,), and in both the Apostles' Creed and the Nicene Creed it is emphasized that Jesus was born of the Virgin Mary.

Objections to the doctrine of the Virgin Birth - more correctly, the virgin conception - are usually based on the fact that it is not mentioned anywhere else in the New Testament (though it has been argued that it is implied by certain of Paul's phrases), and it is claimed that it is a legend based on the Old Testament prophecy, 'Behold, a virgin shall conceive' (Isaiah 7.14 AV), which, in any case, could refer to a young woman who was not necessarily a virgin. Though parthenogenesis, the scientific term for the development of an ovum without fertilization, is known to biology, its occurrence in a human mother could only be the result of divine intervention.

For many Christians the Virgin Birth is an essential part of their faith, a logical consequence of the belief that when Jesus was conceived God entered human history, and a perfect fusion of divine and human elements. (See **Incarnation**) Whether or not people believe that Jesus was born of a virgin, they certainly sing about it in many of the best-known carols*. (See **Ave Maria, Magnificat, Mary**)

Waits Originally the Waits were watchmen, or wakemen, who patrolled the streets during the hours of darkness, calling out the time (e.g. 'Eleven o'clock and all's well!'). They often accompanied this with the ringing of a handbell* and were also known as bellmen. Eventually the Waits began to play musical instruments as a sideline – horns, woodwind, fiddles, bass-viol etc. They used to go round the neighbourhood with their lanterns and instruments during the weeks before Christmas, serenading and also singing carols, with the result that 'the Waits' came to mean a party of carol singers who went from house to house, often being rewarded with gifts of money and festive food* and drink. The ancient Waits of York, who had performed before James I in 1603, were disbanded in 1836 but revived in 1976. (See **Carols**)

Wales (See **Calenigg, Mari Lwyd, Plygain**)

Wartime Christmases Contrary to what might be thought, Christmas during both the First and Second World Wars was not suspended or kept deliberately low-key. Where possible it was celebrated with even more enthusiasm than usual, because – whatever the restrictions, including rationing – it provided a bright interlude in the general gloom of wartime, and was good for keeping up morale.

The Christmases of the First World War (1914-18) were tragic and poignant for the many bereaved families, but a great effort was made to bring cheer and encouragement to the men in the trenches by sending them Christmas cards* and special food* parcels and hampers. (See **Christmas Truce**)

During the Second World War, from 1939, air raids and the blackout added to the unhappy state of families deprived of men and women serving in the armed forces, with millions of children* evacuated. Yet even in areas that had been bombed, there was a determination to celebrate, as shown by the Ministry of Information film *Christmas under Fire.* Throughout the country cards and limited presents were exchanged, carols* were sung, and in spite of rationing (from 1940) traditional dishes were to some extent still served, thanks to saved-up ration coupons and pre-Christmas economy with precious items like sugar, helped by reconstituted dried egg and other alternatives recommended by wartime recipe books. Food was not everything, however, and both in royal broadcasts* and services in church there was a special emphasis on the message of the peace on earth that eventually came in 1945.

Wassail Bowl The old English term 'Wassail' is from the Anglo-Saxon* *Wes hal!*, literally 'Be thou whole!' (i.e. 'Good health!'). The pre-Christian custom of passing round a bowl so that each member of the company could drink the health of the others was absorbed into Christmas tradition. The bowl was usually wooden – ash, maple and rosemary*, for example, are referred to in the old wassail songs. The drink was invariably alcoholic, hot and well spiced, usually the mixture known as Lambswool*, which contained roasted apples*.

Wassail bowls were often elaborate and of enormous size, such as the 10-gallon silver-gilt bowl at Jesus College, Oxford, and always carried into the assembled company with some ceremony. Sometimes the wassail bowl was carried in by a party of mummers* led by Father Christmas*, as we know from an engraving showing this at a masque performed at the court of Charles II.

That the Wassail Bowl was still an important feature of the Victorian Christmas is shown by Charles Dickens* in *Pickwick Papers** (1837): 'They sat down by the huge fire of blazing logs to a substantial supper, and a mighty bowl of wassail, something smaller than an ordinary wash-house copper, in which the hot apples were hissing and bubbling with a rich look, and a jolly sound, that were perfectly irresistible.' (See **Apple Wassailing, Wassailing**)

Wassailing Originally the custom of wishing good health, closely associated with the Anglo-Saxon* wassail bowl*. It then came to mean the custom of carrying the bowl as people sang to bring prosperity to cowsheds, fields and orchards. (See **Apple Wassailing**) Later the term 'wassailing' was used to describe the tradition of parties visiting others at Christmas-time with a wassail bowl – usually decorated with ribbons – which they hoped would be filled with ale or cider. They would beg further seasonal treats after the singing of carols* and special wassail songs, such as the one collected in West Yorkshire, beginning with a reference to the evergreen* garlanding of the wassail bough:

> Here we come a-wassailing
> Among the leaves so green.

An old song from Gloucestershire refers both to the content and to the bowl from which the wassail is to be drunk:

> Wassail, wassail all over the town:
> Our toast it is white, our ale it is brown,
> Our bowl it is made of the white maple tree
> With the wassailing bowl we'll drink to thee!

As recently as the first decades of the twentieth century children* in northern England used to go 'wassailing' to beg some little gift of food or money. The boys were dressed as mummers* and the girls carried a cardboard shoe-box, known as a wassail bough or Wessle Bob*, originally a garland of evergreens in which was a doll representing the Christ-child. This custom has given rise to an alternative explanation of this particular use of 'wassailing' or 'wesselling', namely that it referred to the 'vessel', the box used to represent the crib*. (See **Milly Box**)

Watchnight The Watchnight service, designed to usher in the New Year*, was introduced amongst the early Methodists in 1742 by John Wesley, who claimed he was simply reviving the prayer vigils held by the Early Church. The service starts late on New Year's Eve, and may include Communion. It is essentially a time of heart-searching and spiritual renewal, typified by the words of a hymn by Charles Wesley, traditionally started on the first stroke of midnight, beginning:

> Come, let us anew
> Our journey pursue,
> Roll round with the year,
> And never stand still till the Master appear.

Christians of several other denominations have now adopted the Watchnight service, which sometimes appears as one of the New Year programmes on television.

Wenceslas Familiar through J.M. Neale's fanciful Victorian carol* as 'Good King Wenceslas', who went out into the deep snow and cruel frost of the Feast of Stephen* (i.e. Boxing Day*) to offer hospitality to a poor man 'gathering winter fuel'. Neale seems to have had little or no historical basis for this particular story, but Wenceslas was indeed a king with a reputation for charitable acts of this sort. Grandson of St Ludmilla, he became King of Bohemia in 922 AD, when he was only fifteen. Probably because of his work to strengthen ties with western countries he was murdered by his brother Boleslav in 929, and soon became venerated as a martyr and saint. Wenceslas is buried in the Church of St Vitus in Prague and is the patron saint of Czechoslovakia.

161

Wessle-Bob, Wesley Bob A corruption of Wassail Bob, this term was also used in Yorkshire to mean baubles* for a Christmas tree*. (See **Wassailing)**

While shepherds watched One of the best-loved of the older carols*, this was written by the Irish Protestant minister Nahum Tate (1652-1715), who in 1692 became Poet Laureate. It has the distinction of being the first carol to gain official approval for use in church services, because it is a close paraphrase of the account of the nativity* in St Luke's Gospel. It is usually sung to Winchester Old, but other tunes used are Lyngham, Christmas Bells and Cranbrook, the tune that is now associated with the Yorkshire dialect song 'On Ilkla Mooar baht 'at', but still occasionally used for this particular carol.

White Christmas This is the classic Christmas of popular imagination, with scenes of snowmen, snowballing, sledging and skating. A Christmas when there is a covering of snow – or even a substantial hoar-frost – is a comparatively rare event in Britain, though it was more common before 1752, when the calendar was changed, moving Christmas back by about eleven days. Even in Dickensian times Christmases were much colder, the extensive white Christmas of 1836, for example, providing the background for *Pickwick Papers**. Although snow has fallen on Christmas Day itself only about ten times in the past 100 years, snowfalls are reasonably likely at some point during the Twelve Days of Christmas* in spite of global warming. (See **Christmas Day**)

White Christmas (Song) 'I'm dreaming of a White Christmas' by Irving Berlin, sung by Bing Crosby, is the best-selling gramophone record of all time. Composed in 1941, it was released just before the film in which it first features, *Holiday Inn,* in October 1942, and by the end of the year had sold a million copies. In 1960 Bing Crosby was presented by Decca with a golden disc of 'White Christmas' to celebrate the total sale of 200 million records.

Winter Solstice The shortest day in the year – in the northern hemisphere 21 or 22 December – and the focal point of many ancient ceremonies and festivals. As autumn merged into winter, when the feeble sun had reached its lowest point in the sky, various superstitious practices were designed to strengthen it, especially the lighting of great fires and the burning of lights. The survivals of these ancient festivals of light and fire can be clearly seen in the Romans'* Saturnalia* and the Yule-tide and Queen of Light* festivals in Scandinavia*, and also in the importance of fire and light in so many Christmas traditions.

Whatever the earliest ceremonies were it seemed to the primitive mind that they really had been effective, because soon after 21/22 December it was observed that the sun was beginning to rise higher and that the days were getting longer. Since the ceremony appeared to have worked it was repeated with unfailing regularity at every winter solstice.

The festivals connected with the winter solstice tended to last many days, some from the end of November well into January. In addition to their superstitious, magical nature they were an attempt to brighten up the gloomy winter, and it is no coincidence that Christmas also occurs at this time of the year. 21 December is actually St Thomas's Day, a time when it was traditional to give charitable* gifts of food* and money etc. (See **Christmas, Christmas Day, Druids, Hogmanay, Saint Thomas, Saturnalia, Sword Dancing, Up-Helly-Aa, Yule-tide**)

Wise Men Popularly known as 'the three wise men' or 'the three kings', these famous visitors, guided to the Christ-child by a star, are mentioned only in St Matthew's account of the nativity* (Matthew 2.1-12). Nowhere in this account, however, does he say that there were three of them – an assumption made from the statement that they presented three gifts: gold*, frankincense* and myrrh*. Nor does he say that they were kings, though this idea gains some support from the fact that their presents were expensive and that the visitors were received with some deference by treacherous King Herod*. The first suggestion that they were kings was made by Tertullian (160-220 AD), and although this idea was eagerly taken up by artists it is now generally agreed that they were philosophers or priests from Babylon or Persia, well versed in the study of the heavens, hence some modern translations giving 'astrologers' for Matthew's term *magoi*.

Whoever they were, the Wise Men were certainly not Jews, and the significance of their visit is that homage was paid to the Jewish Messiah* by Gentiles, an event commemorated by Epiphany* which is observed on 6 January. At Epiphany it has long been traditional for the king or queen of England to present token gifts of gold, frankincense and myrrh in the Chapel Royal, St James' Palace. Nowadays two Gentlemen Ushers do it on the Queen's* behalf, 25 sovereigns distributed to pensioners, frankincense to the Church and myrrh to the Hospital.

The first known written reference to *three* Wise Men was made by Origen (185-254 AD) but it is not until the sixth century that we come across their traditional names of Melchior*, Kaspar* and Balthasar*. Their bones, or at least their skulls, were said to have been preserved as holy relics, brought from Constantinople to Milan (fifth century) then taken to Germany* (twelfth century), where they are now in a golden, bejewelled shrine, which can be seen above the high altar of Cologne Cathedral. Richard II was born at Epiphany 1367, and is shown in a famous triptych as one of the Three Wise Men at Bethlehem*.

Much has been made of the legendary 'fourth' Wise Man, who is said to have arrived to see Jesus only in time for the crucifixion, because he had spent so much time on the journey doing good works. (See **Fourth Wise Man**, **Magi**, **Star of Bethlehem**)

Wishbone Once also referred to as the 'Merry-thought', this is the forked bone at the front of the breastbone of poultry, especially turkey*, which is used for an old and familiar custom. Two people each loop a little finger round one fork of the wishbone, then make a wish as they pull. It is usual to pretend that the one who has the larger piece will have the wish granted.

Woden An alternative name for Odin, the form used by the Scandinavians*. Woden was the name the Anglo-Saxons* used, and is preserved in our word Wednesday – Woden's Day. (See **Odin**)

Wreaths A custom, originally observed during the Roman* festival of Saturnalia*, is the practice of attaching a wreath of evergreens to the outside of the front door, as an indication of welcome during the festive season. It is also customary to place a smaller, less elaborate wreath on the grave of someone especially remembered at Christmas-time. (See **Advent Wreath, Evergreens**)

Wren The diminutive and especially appealing Jenny Wren, the 'King of the Birds', was once the subject of many legends, and the object of a strange Christmas custom. On St Stephen's Day (Boxing Day*) country lads went out 'hunting the Wren'. This day is thought to have been chosen because when St Stephen was in hiding from his persecutors a wren was supposed to have betrayed his presence by its loud singing.

In a few areas the wren was caught, put in a special cage adorned with ribbons, carried round the district, then released. In others it was caught and killed, then tied to the end of a long, decorated pole and carried round in triumph by the Wren Boys, who sang, danced and collected money, often for charity*. This curiously barbaric custom survived longest in Wales*, the Isle of Man and Southern Ireland. A pleasanter tradition is the myth that the wren brought moss and feathers to make a covering for the baby Jesus* in the manger*.

Xmas An abbreviated form of the word Christmas, which is incorrectly assumed to be modern and secular, so much so that some people object to it as a slick, commercial name, deliberately excluding 'Christ'*. Yet 'Xmas' is, in fact, of ancient origin, the X being the Greek 'Ch' in the original spelling of Christ in the New Testament. The letter was used over a thousand years ago in the *Anglo-Saxon* Chronicle*, and was still an accepted and reverent abbreviation in Victorian times. For example, the artist who designed the first Christmas card signed his personal copies: 'J.C. Horsley*, Xmasse, 1843'. So 'Xmas', far from being a modern way of leaving Christ out of Christmas, is actually an old-fashioned way of keeping him there in the original spelling.

York Minster York was one of the most northerly outposts of the early Christian world and its beautiful minster retains an ancient custom which probably derives from the conversion of Celtic and Scandinavian* tribes to Christianity. A large sprig of mistletoe*, originally an entirely pagan symbol, was carried in procession and placed on the high altar of York Minster on Christmas Eve. It was left there throughout the Twelve Days of Christmas*, and during this period a general pardon was proclaimed in the city. A notable exception to the usual banning of mistletoe in churches, this custom seemed to symbolize the triumph of Christianity over paganism. Moreover, it is still maintained, the Dean of York ceremonially tying bunches of mistletoe to the riddleposts of the altar at 12 noon every Christmas Eve.

Yule, Yule-tide One of the ancient pre-Christian festivals, held at the time of the winter solstice*. It was observed by the northern races, mainly the Anglo-Saxons* and Scandinavians, and its name is probably derived from the Norse word for the shortest day in the year. It was originally a festival intended to revive the dying sun and celebrate its return, but later became associated with the gods of Viking mythology such as Odin* (Woden*), Thor and Freya. It was a 'grith-day', when everyone was at peace, brightening up the winter with evergreen decorations, great bonfires and the burning of a yule-log*, to the accompaniment of feasting, the drinking of mead* and the exchange of gifts.

Like the Roman* festival of Saturnalia* Yule-tide was gradually absorbed into the Christian celebrations of the birth of Jesus*, and in England the term Yule-tide became synonymous with Christmas, especially during the reign of Alfred the Great (849-99). (See **Boar's Head, Scandinavia, Up-Helly-Aa**)

Yule-bread, **Yule-cakes** Various forms of Christmas cake*, made to rise by the inclusion of yeast, these contained dried fruit* and spices*, and were popular in country districts, especially in northern parts of Britain, where yule-cakes were sometimes small and served individually.

Yule-candle A large candle which was traditionally lit by the master of the house on Christmas Eve and allowed to burn through the night, and sometimes throughout the Twelve Days of Christmas*. It was considered unlucky to light any other candle from it, and a very bad omen for the family if it went out. The custom dates back to at least the time of King Alfred and was mentioned as quite usual in the diary of Parson Woodforde, writing in Norfolk in 1790. A particularly large yule-candle used to be placed on the high table at St John's College, Oxford and allowed to burn for all the Twelve Days of Christmas. The ancient stone candle-holder used for the purpose is still preserved in the college buttery. (See **Candles**)

Yule-log The ceremonial burning of a log (or smaller piece known as a Yule Clog) at the time of the winter solstice* is one of the most ancient of customs, and is especially associated with the Anglo-Saxon* and Scandinavian* festival of Yule-tide*. Its origin is probably the even older ritual of lighting a great fire to revive the dying sun, and the idea of preserving the continuity of life is seen in the custom – still practised in some country districts – of lighting the yule-log with a charred fragment that has been kept from the log burnt the previous year.

Until comparatively recently, in the days when fireplaces were large enough, it was customary to bring in the yule-log with great ceremony on Christmas Eve. The log was a carefully selected trunk, ideally of oak or ash, and better still if it had mistletoe* growing in the branches of the tree. It was felled, trimmed and dragged from the forest in style, decorated with ribbons and evergreens, and greeted by all who had the good fortune to see the procession. It had to be large enough to burn through at least Christmas Day and, if possible, right through the Twelve Days of Christmas*. Occasionally it was rekindled at Candlemas*. In some districts ale or cider was sprinkled on the log before it was lit. In Cornwall it was known as the 'Christmas Block' (or 'Mock') and the figure of a man was chalked on it, perhaps a faint reminiscence of prehistoric human sacrifice by fire. In the Scottish Highlands it used to be the custom to carve the figure of an old woman from a small tree-stump. This was known as the *Cailleach nollaich*, the 'Christmas Old

Wife', a symbolic representation of evil and misfortune, which was ceremonially burnt on the peat fire.

Many pre-Christian superstitions were associated with the yule-log. The person lighting it was specially chosen and had to make sure his or her hands were well-washed. While the log burnt no one with bare feet or any deformity was supposed to enter the room. It was never allowed to burn away completely, and not only was a fragment saved for kindling the log the following year, but the charcoal and ashes were kept for use as magical charms. (See also **Ashen Faggot, Bûche de Noël**)

Zampognari Italian shepherds in costume, who act as the heralds of Christmas by coming into the towns to play their huge bagpipes, especially before images and statues of the Madonna* and Child.

Zinzendorf Count Nicholas von Zinzendorf, founder of the Moravians, did much to encourage the celebration of Christmas outside his native Germany*, in particular, in the town called Bethlehem* in Pennsylvania, where he held a service in a stable on Christmas Eve 1741.

Zwarte Piet (See **Holland**)

Zygocactus The plant popularly known as the Christmas Cactus is botanically either *Zygocatus truncatus* (also called *Schlumbergera truncata*), or a similar *Schlumbergera* species. It originally grew only in Brazil, but has been cultivated in European homes for nearly 200 years. It can be one of the most beautiful of Christmas decorations*, producing on mature plants many double blooms of bright magenta pink (100 on the author's 40-year-old specimen) which can be timed to be at their best on Christmas Day itself.

The Christmas Cactus thrives in moist, peaty compost, similar to the damp material it grows on in the forks of trees or in pockets in the rocks in the foothills of Rio de Janeiro. It does well in warm shady conditions, but is best placed outdoors in full sun between June and September, when it should be well watered and given a little liquid fertilizer, though in the colder months it should be watered very sparingly. The Christmas Cactus is easily propagated from cuttings.

For Further Reading

W. Irving, *The Sketch Book* (1818).
W. Hone, *The Every-Day Book* (1827).
C. Dickens, *A Christmas Carol* (1843).
C.C. Moore, *A Visit from St Nicholas* (1848).
J. Brand, *Observations on Popular Antiquities* (1849).
R. Chambers, *The Book of Days* (1878).
T.K. Harvey, *The Book of Christmas* (1888).
J.G. Frazer, *The Golden Bough* (1922).
J. Fairfax-Blakeborough, *Wit, Character, Folklore, Customs etc.* (1898).
A.R. Wright, *British Calendar Customs* (1938).
M. Harrison, *The Story of Christmas* (1951).
J.H. Barnett, *The American Christmas* (1954).
Dylan Thomas, *A Child's Christmas in Wales* (1954).
C. Hole, *Christmas and its Customs* (1957).
M. and J. Hadfield, *The Twelve Days of Christmas* (1961).
M. Baker, *Christmas Customs and Folklore* (1968).
H. Loxton, ed., *Christmas* (1970).
E. Walter, ed., *A Christmas Scrapbook* (1979).
F. and J. Muir, *A Treasury of Christmas* (1981).
M. Brown, S. Seaton, *The Christmas Truce* (1984).
J.M. Golby, A.W. Purdue, *The Making of the Modern Christmas* (1984).
D. Byrne, *Israel and the Holy Land* (1985).
R. Brownrigg, *Come, See the Place* (1985).
J. Smith, *Fairs, Feasts and Frolics* (1989).
M. and A. Hubert, *A Wartime Christmas* (1995)
J. Matthews, *The Winter Solstice – Sacred Traditions of Christmas* (1998).
A. Kellett, *Kellett's Christmas* (1998).
I. Bradley, ed., *The Penguin Book of Carols* (1999).
G. Bowler, *The World Encyclopedia of Christmas* (2000).
J. Simpson, S. Roud, *The Oxford Dictionary of English Folklore* (2000).
A. Kellett, *Mother Shipton* (2002).
A. Kellett, *Yorkshire Dictionary of Dialect, Tradition and Folklore* (2002).
P. Harding, *Christmas Unwrapped* (2002).
P. Kimpton, *Tom Smith's Christmas Crackers* (2004).
M. Deeprose, *The Pitkin Guide to Carols* (including CD)(2005).

Interesting material can also be seen on the internet site of Maria von Staufer's *Christmas Archives*. (www.christmasarchives.com)